THE LANGUAGE MACHINE

The Language Machine

Roy Harris
Professor of General Linguistics
in the University of Oxford

Duckworth

First published in 1987 by
Gerald Duckworth & Co. Ltd.
The Old Piano Factory
43 Gloucester Crescent, London NW1

ISBN 0 7156 2172 6

British Library Cataloguing in Publication Data

Harris, Roy, *1931–*
    The language machine.
    1. Language and languages   2. Communication
    I. Title
    400   P90

    ISBN 0-7156-2172-6

Photoset in North Wales by
Derek Doyle & Associates, Mold, Clwyd
and printed in Great Britain by
The Alden Press, Oxford

Contents

I cannot think it will ever be safe to repose much trust in the moral sense of any machine

Samuel Butler

Preface

The language myth of post-Renaissance European culture presents languages as fixed codes which enable individuals to communicate their thoughts to one another by means of words, and portrays linguistic communities as groups of individuals who use the same language. This is a myth which defines communication between human beings as thought transference, and then postulates a social institution (the language) which makes that possible. It is a myth which has its intellectual roots in the Western tradition, its political basis in the European nation-state, and which drew its original psychological support from the revolution ushered in by one of the most important inventions in human history: printing. It is the language myth of a literate culture in which the major linguistic divisions correspond roughly to national boundaries and the most advanced communications technology is typography.

It is essentially a language myth which ignores differences between individuals, in favour of emphasising collective conformities. In so doing it generates an internal problem of its own. Since, from the cradle to the grave, the personal linguistic history of every individual is unique, how is it possible that this rich variety of linguistic experience at the individual level should ever give rise to a common language of the kind which the myth postulates? How does linguistic unity emerge from linguistic diversity?

Mythical problems demand mythical solutions. The solution in this case lay in constructing a supporting explanatory mythology, according to which Nature prudently foresaw the difficulty and provided the answer in advance. The answer turns out to be that *homo sapiens* is a creature uniquely endowed with a special apparatus in the brain, genetically designed to perform the miracle of constructing communal linguistic systems. Thus the species comes fully equipped with the means of solving all the basic communicational problems prejudicial to its survival.

7

Individual linguistic disparities are transformed into collective linguistic uniformities by a biological language machine within us. We do not need to make languages. The machine makes them for us, whatever the circumstances. A more felicitous collaboration between Nature and Nurture could scarcely be imagined.

The mythology of this remarkable and mysterious language machine supplies the following chapters with their theme. It is a theme whose historical evolution reflects the passage from the typographical culture in which the problem originally arose to the electronic culture of the present day. In its contemporary form it is overtly a computer-age mythology, taking for granted that machines can 'handle language' while conveniently ignoring the question of what exactly it is that machines do with the 'language' they 'handle'. It is a mythology which merits critical scrutiny for many reasons; not least because its acceptance has contributed so powerfully to what has aptly been called the 'exorcism of mind from science'.

Introduction

Linguistics in Lagado

A *New Yorker* cartoon of 1958 shows two small worried men standing beside an enormous computer-type apparatus. They are reading the message on a reel of paper tape issuing forth from an orifice in the machine's vast, dial-studded bulk. The caption is: 'I'll be damned. It says, "*Cogito, ergo sum*".' The intellectual history of this cartoon, or rather of the idea to which it gives expression, is of considerable interest in the context of the development of Western thinking about language.

The cartoon was subsequently reproduced as the frontispiece of a volume of papers on problems of cognition contributed by a number of eminent philosophers, published under the appropriate title *Minds and Machines*.[1] In that particular context, it is difficult not to see the two small worried men of the cartoon as representatives of the philosophers of the Western post-Socratic tradition. For in that philosophical tradition, the ability to handle language has always been regarded as the distinguishing characteristic of beings possessing minds. From Isocrates down to Descartes, language was taken to be not merely beyond the capacity of inanimate objects, but an eternal divide separating mankind from other living species. This criterion underlies the Cartesian notion of *la bête machine*, which demotes animals to the status of mere mechanisms, even though their behaviour appears superficially to resemble that of human beings in certain striking respects. The criterion was reaffirmed in the nineteenth century by those critics of Darwin who agreed with Oxford's first Professor of Comparative Philology when he claimed on behalf of the human race that 'Language is our Rubicon, and no brute will dare to cross it'.[2] It goes without saying that for his generation

[1] Ed. A.R.Anderson, Englewood Cliffs 1964.
[2] F.M.Müller, *Lectures on the Science of Language*, London 1861, p.340.

9

language was also a Rubicon which would keep the machine out as well as the brute, insofar as there was any distinction between the two.

The *New Yorker* cartoon is doubly ironic inasmuch as the appeal of the argument *Cogito, ergo sum* had always relied implicitly upon the conviction that words themselves were evidence of thought. Hence being able to formulate the very words *Cogito, ergo sum* stood as a demonstration that any being capable of this formulation must be right in claiming to be able to think, and therefore establishing by that fact alone the truth of the proposition *Cogito*.

If this holds for human beings, why not for machines? But then, unfortunately, the presumed superiority of the human being over the machine is automatically (in more than one sense) cancelled out. 'I'll be damned. It says, *"Cogito, ergo sum"*.' can be read as: 'Either we've built a machine which can think just as well as we do; or else we have proved that we are only machines ourselves.' Both horns of the dilemma are equally sharp, and the dilemma arises from the role tacitly attributed to language.

* * *

If it is accepted that only minds can reason, that only living creatures have minds, and that language is the hallmark of rationality, then no idea is more subversive – not to say self-contradictory – than the idea of a language machine. It is no surprise to find, therefore, that when the idea of a language machine makes its first appearance in Western literature, the literary purpose it serves is that of satire. The satirist is Swift and the work in question is *Gulliver's Travels*. When Gulliver visited the grand academy at Lagado he was invited to inspect a curious research project, of which he gives the following remarkable account.[3]

> We crossed a walk to the other part of the academy, where, as I have already said, the projectors in speculative learning resided. The first professor I saw was in a very large room, with forty pupils about him. After salutation, observing me to look earnestly upon a frame, which took up the greatest part of both the length and breadth of the room; he said, perhaps I might wonder to see him

[3] *Gulliver's Travels*, Part III, Ch.V.

employed in a project for improving speculative knowledge by practical and mechanical operations. But the world would soon be sensible of its usefulness; and he flattered himself, that a more noble exalted thought never sprang in any other man's head. Every one knew how laborious the usual method is of attaining to arts and sciences; whereas by his contrivance, the most ignorant person at a reasonable charge, and with a little bodily labour, may write books in philosophy, poetry, politicks, law, mathematicks and theology, without the least assistance from genius or study. He then led me to a frame, about the sides whereof all his pupils stood in ranks. It was twenty foot square, placed in the middle of the room. The superficies was composed of several bits of wood, about the bigness of a dye, but some larger than others. They were all linked together by slender wires. These bits of wood were covered on every square with paper pasted on them; and, on these papers were written all the words of their language in their several moods, tenses and declensions, but without any order. The professor then desired me to observe, for he was going to set his engine at work. The pupils at his command took each of them hold of an iron handle, whereof there were forty fixed round the edges of the frame; and giving them a sudden turn, the whole disposition of the words was entirely changed. He then commanded six and thirty of the lads to read the several lines softly as they appeared upon the frame; and where they found three or four words together that might make part of a sentence, they dictated to the four remaining boys who were scribes. This work was repeated three or four times, and at every turn the engine was so contrived, that the words shifted into new places, as the square bits of wood moved upside down.

Six hours a-day the young students were employed in this labour; and the professor shewed me several volumes in large folio already collected, of broken sentences, which he intended to piece together; and out of those rich materials to give the world a compleat body of all arts and sciences; which, however might be still improved, and much expedited, if the publick would raise a fund for the making and employing five hundred such frames in Lagado, and oblige the managers to contribute in common their several collections.

He assured me that this invention had employed all his thoughts from his youth; that he had emptied the whole vocabulary into his frame, and made the strictest computation of the general proportion there is in books between the numbers of particles, nouns, and verbs, and other parts of speech.

I made my humblest acknowledgements to this illustrious person for his great communicativeness; and promised, if ever I had the good fortune to return to my native country, that I would do him justice, as the sole inventor of this wonderful machine; the form and contrivance of which I desired leave to delineate upon paper as in the figure here annexed. I told him, although it were the custom of our learned in Europe to steal inventions from each other, who had thereby at least this advantage, that it became a controversy which was the right owner; yet I would take such caution, that he should have the honour entire without a rival.

Here for the first time we see explicit recognition that the concept of a language and the concept of a machine are related in a particular way. On the one hand, there is recognition that language involves operations of a syntactic kind which are purely mechanical. On the other hand, there is recognition that machines are devices of which the output can be described in terms which do not differ essentially from those applied in assessing certain levels of human linguistic ability. These two realisations are head and tail of the same coin. Swift happens to have been the first writer to embody that connexion in a specific, although speculative, metaphor. His language machine of Lagado both gave that metaphor a concrete literary status and established a landmark in Western thinking about language.

The idea of a language machine, like all influential ideas, did not spring fully armed into the mind of Swift or anyone else. Long before the publication of *Gulliver's Travels* people had speculated about the mechanisation of various mental processes. Contrivances that produce speech had a venerable history in the folklore of science long before modern toymakers managed to produce the first talking doll, and even before von Kempelen made his pioneering artificial vocal apparatus at the end of the eighteenth century. In the Middle Ages, Roger Bacon, Albertus Magnus and Pope Sylvester II were all credited with the invention of various robot devices capable of uttering words. The origins of the notion of a 'talking apparatus' can be traced back to tales of the oracular statues of ancient Egypt, Greece and Assyria.[4] Attempts to mechanise counting go back at least as far as the invention of the abacus, and came to fruition when Pascal designed the first calculating machine. Leibniz's dream of a reasoning machine was inspired by the earlier contrivance devised by Ramon Lull in which words arranged in concentric circles supplied automatic answers when other words were arranged to form questions. The first we hear of an attempt to

---

[4] J.Cohen, *Human Robots in Myth and Science*, London 1966, Ch.1.

mechanise the production of word-sequences in general does, however, come from Swift's account of the grand academy of Lagado. It is the first account on record of anything that might reasonably be called a 'language laboratory'.

What Swift could hardly have foreseen when he wrote *Gulliver's Travels* is that some two hundred years later scientists would be seriously engaged in research projects aiming at the construction of machines no less ambitious than the machine Gulliver inspected: machines which would produce speech, machines which would recognise speech, and machines which would translate from one language into another. Nor could he have anticipated that the language machine of Lagado might begin to look like a prophetic parody of claims about language which were subsequently to achieve respectability in twentieth-century linguistics. The patent absurdity of the scientific enterprises conducted at the grand academy of Lagado may at first sight obscure the similarities between the theory of linguistic structure on which the academy's language machine is based and that which underlies much more recent attempts to explain the workings of language in the human mind. According to many contemporary theorists, the crucial mental difference between *homo sapiens* and all other living species is precisely that only *homo sapiens* is equipped with a language machine in the brain. The postulated machine in the brain is, needless to say, a much improved version of the crude prototype at Lagado: it is, specifically, a device which generates sentences instead of word salad. This internal sentence-generator, which human beings alone have, is held to be the key to the whole range of mankind's various linguistic activities.

Trying to build machines to do what at one time only human beings could do, thereby saving the necessity for human effort, is one of the most constant and conspicuous preoccupations of our species. So much so that it would be remarkable if in the course of civilisation no philosopher had come to the view that human beings themselves are just highly intricate machines.

Furthermore, if human beings are indeed machines, as mechanistic philosophers have held, it seems plausible that anything a human being can do will turn out eventually to be something which can, in principle, be mechanically produced in a laboratory, using non-biological materials. The most convincing validation of the mechanistic doctrine of man would no doubt be to construct a robot which could do everything a human being could do. To attempt this straight off would be a tall order; but the task seems more manageable if broken down into a series of attempts to design separate machines for separate purposes. To each and every human capacity there would thus correspond a possible machine. Even if, owing to current limitations of technology, it were not possible to build these machines, it should none the less be possible to go some way towards blueprints for them: in other words, to specify on paper the mechanical form a particular machine should have if it were to be able to match a given human capacity. The assumptions about the human capacity for language which underlie some of the most important developments which have taken place in linguistic theory in the twentieth century are essentially mechanistic assumptions. The link between Lagado and modern linguistics is not fortuitous.

The first published treatise to argue the case that the human being is simply a machine was La Mettrie's *L'homme machine* of 1747. The first to present the case, even tentatively, that some machines are (in all essentials) capable of becoming human was Simons's *Are Computers Alive?* of 1983. The time span separating the two is interesting. It apparently took almost two and a half centuries to bridge the gap between the two not very dissimilar ideas that (i) everything human beings can do machines could – in principle – do too, and (ii) that machines, having the same potential as human beings, ought to be recognised as (potential) human beings. The reason for the gap is not difficult to find. Clearly the cultural and psychological potential of the two ideas, and the kind of resistance they were to produce, was very different. Why?

Part of the answer is that La Mettrie's thesis did not require any technological back-up in order to make it into a challenge which the established religious orthodoxy of his day had to recognise and take seriously. The complementary thesis that machines may become human, on the other hand, did not constitute a challenge which had to be taken seriously by anyone until technology had advanced to the point of making the actual construction of such machines seem both feasible and imminent. Having to wait for the computer revolution, however, is not the whole story. La Mettrie's thesis, unpopular as it was when first advanced, offered a new mode of explanation for certain forms of human behaviour; or at least appeared to do so. In this respect, La Mettrie already had the history of science on his side.

Human beings have always supposed that they had an adequate understanding of machines, the proof of the understanding being simply that human beings could make machines and make them work. Hence, discovering progressively throughout history that more and more parts of the universe could be treated as working on purely mechanical principles had always seemed to constitute a cumulative advance in scientific knowledge. A remark much quoted in this connexion is Lord Kelvin's: 'If I can make a mechanical model, I can understand it. As long as I cannot make a mechanical model all the way through, I cannot understand it.'

Just the opposite, on the other hand, might seem to follow from the far more radically subversive thesis that machines could be made human. Instead of reducing the unknown to the known, elevating a computer to the level of a quasi-human or even superhuman intelligence goes against the grain of a whole epistemology. It suggests that machines, beyond a certain level of complexity, are just as mysterious as human beings, and perhaps therefore just as unpredictable. This poses a double threat. First, it undermines the time-honoured equation between the mechanical and the knowable. Second, it evokes the alarming prospect that more intelligent machines might eventually enslave their human makers. Machines are acceptable to humanity only as long as they remain strictly under human control. The possibility of a human race one day controlled by machines is an idea in itself so repugnant that it has to be relegated to the realms of science fiction.

Linguistics in Swift's Lagado invites direct comparison – at least, for twentieth-century readers – with linguistics in Orwell's Oceania. What Swift satirised as an absurdity was conceded by Orwell to be an ominously impending reality. The world of *Nineteen Eighty-Four* has already progressed technologically to the automatic production of texts. Swift's professor has been replaced by the officials of the Ministry of Truth,

> ...whose primary job was not to reconstruct the past but to supply the citizens of Oceania with newspapers, films, textbooks, telescreen programmes, plays, novels – with every conceivable kind of information, instruction, or entertainment, from a statute to a slogan, from a lyric poem to a biological treatise, and from a

child's spelling-book to a Newspeak dictionary. And the Ministry had not only to supply the multifarious needs of the Party, but also to repeat the whole operation at a lower level for the benefit of the proletariat. There was a whole chain of departments dealing with proletarian literature, music, drama, and entertainment generally. Here were produced rubbishy newspapers containing almost nothing except sport, crime and astrology, sensational five-cent novelettes, films oozing with sex, and sentimental songs which were composed entirely by mechanical means on a special kind of kaleidoscope known as a versificator.[5]

In the years since Orwell published *Nineteen Eighty-Four*, the versificator has become reality, and its products are by no means limited to the trash which Orwell had in mind. Orwell's facile equation of the mechanical with the trite here rebounds upon the prophet of linguistic doom. Precisely what mechanical versificators seem to be good at is hitting upon unexpected combinations of words with poetic potential; and this is doubtless because they are not limited by the ingrained run-of-the-mill verbal associations which hamper the human poet. By comparison with the versificator, it turns out to be the flesh-and-blood versifier who is 'mechanical'. (One can hardly hold against the machine that it produces more 'bad' poems than 'good' ones: for that criticism presupposes that the excellence of a Shakespeare or a Keats has somehow to be judged by the number of drafts that were consigned to the wastepaper basket.)

Why Orwell limited mechanical text production in Oceania to the lyrics of sentimental songs is not at all clear in the context of *Nineteen Eighty-Four*. Elsewhere, as W.F.Bolton points out, Orwell conceded that 'it probably would not be beyond human ingenuity to write books by machinery'.[6] This is an illuminating concession on more than one count. Since Orwell was well acquainted with *Gulliver's Travels*, his admission that books might be written by machinery is tantamount to saying, with historical hindsight, that Swift got it wrong. But in Orwell's day no feat of human ingenuity had come anywhere near writing a book by machinery. It was no more a practical proposition for Orwell's publishers than it had been for Swift's. So if we are to look for the reason why Orwell found this credible whereas Swift

[5] G.Orwell, *Nineteen Eighty-Four*, London 1949, p.38.
[6] S.Orwell and I.Angus (eds.), *The Collected Essays, Journalism and Letters of George Orwell*, London 1968, vol.4, p.71.

found it ludicrous, it will be no use pointing to advances in the *de facto* mechanisation of book-writing: for there were none. The answer is to be sought in the assumptions about language which underlie that no less famous figment of Orwellian linguistics: the invention of Newspeak.

Newspeak is a deliberately distorted and restricted language, designed to ensure the political enslavement of its speakers. The objective, as Orwell describes it, is not merely that opposition to the Party should have no readily available form of expression, but that thoughts not approved by the Party 'should be literally unthinkable'. The horrendous and masterly postscript to the novel, where we are told the details of the programme by which Newspeak will eventually replace Oldspeak entirely, rivals anything to be found in the pages of Swift. That final vision of how the deliberate manipulation of language could make freedom of thought impossible remains one of the most chillingly powerful in the whole of English literature.

Commentators have not been slow to point out how much there is in common between Swift's sallies into speculative linguistics and Orwell's. The crude truncations of Newspeak are foreshadowed by another research project at Lagado, which aimed to improve the Balnibarbian language 'by cutting polysyllables into one, and leaving out verbs and participles'.[7] Already in the *Voyage to the Houyhnhms* we find the notion of a language which exists solely in order to represent a perceived version of the truth, and which consequently has no words for 'lying' or 'falsehood'. More significant than the similarities of detail between Swift and Orwell, however, are the differences in attitude. Both writers were familiar with Utopian linguistic proposals of various kinds (Bishop Wilkins's 'real character'; C.K.Ogden's 'Basic English'). But whereas 'Swift is ambiguous in his evaluation of these imaginary languages ... in Orwell the Utopian ideal of a unified factual language has become dystopian'.[8]

That evaluative shift would be inexplicable, and Newspeak a nonsense rather than a menace, unless supported by two typically twentieth-century assumptions. One is that human linguistic abilities depend on a language machine in the brain.

---

[7] *Gulliver's Travels*, Part III, Ch.V.

[8] P.Chilton, 'Orwell, language and linguistics', *Language & Communication*, vol.4, 1984, p.130.

18   *The Language Machine*

The other is that once the language machine is programmed in a certain way, the individual is powerless to alter it. The machine restricts the individual's forms of expression and channels the processes of thought. That is evidently the linguistic theory held by Orwell's sinister experts at the Ministry of Truth: and unless that theory had some ring of presumptive plausibility for modern readers, the bleak vision of a Newspeak society would immediately lose its chill. Orwell, unlike Swift, was writing for a generation already half-prepared to accept that human beings might be unwitting intellectual prisoners of their own language. The other side of the coin is that if Swift had portrayed a grand academy whose Professor of Glottomechanics had access to computer technology, few readers in the second half of the twentieth century would see anything absurd in the project of writing books in Balnibarbian by machine.

This is not because in practice we are accustomed to machines writing our books for us, but because between Swift's generation and our own there has been a revolutionary change in the relationship between the concepts of what is characteristically mechanical and what is characteristically human. A major landmark here is A.M.Turing's famous paper on 'Computing Machines and Intelligence',[9] and it is still a landmark which is essential for taking one's bearings in this area. Turing's argument constitutes the watershed dividing those currents of thought which flow back to Descartes' view of mind from those which flow forward towards Searle's contention that *'only* a machine could think'.[10]

Turing draws an extended analogy between computation as undertaken by a human being and computation as undertaken by a machine. The human being, he says, is supposed to be 'following fixed rules' and has 'no authority to deviate from them in any detail'.[11] Turing distinguishes between the rules and the actual calculations which the human being carries out. Here, evidently, he is thinking of the difference between, say, someone's calculating the product of 243 × 187 and the arithmetic on which such a calculation is based. Now

[9] Originally published in *Mind*, vol.LIX, no.236, 1950. Reprinted in Anderson, op. cit. Page references are to the reprint.

[10] J.R.Searle, 'Minds, brains and programs', *The Behavioral and Brain Sciences*, vol.3, 1980, pp.418-57.

[11] Turing, op. cit., p.8.

calculations, according to Turing, can be done in two ways. You can do them on paper or you can do them 'in your head'. (He does not mention other possibilities, such as using an abacus or matchsticks, although it is difficult to suppose that this omission is an oversight on his part.) For Turing, doing calculations 'in your head' requires something equivalent to a supply of paper, and this mental supply of paper is – memory.

Memory also, on Turing's analogy, has another paper-like function: it is required for recording the 'book of rules' which governs the calculation itself. In practice, we do not need recourse to any real book in order to carry out, say, the steps of a simple multiplication, in the way a cook might need to consult a recipe book in preparing a dish. In fact, the 'book of rules' is what Turing calls 'a convenient fiction': for in everyday cases human beings 'really remember what they have got to do'.[12]

This is Turing's account of human computation. How about computation by machine? The machine also needs something corresponding to a book of rules, and this Turing calls a 'table of instructions'. The machine's table of instructions is located in what is called its 'store'. The store is a 'store of information', which in turn corresponds to the human being's paper, which in turn corresponds to the human memory insofar as computation is carried out 'in your head'. The machine's store is different from its 'executive unit', which is 'the part which carries out the various individual operations involved in a calculation'. The machine's executive unit, therefore, is responsible for carrying out a typical instruction such as:

Add the number stored in position 6809 to that in 4302 and put the result back into the latter storage position.

A typical instruction of this kind would not, says Turing, 'occur in the machine expressed in English'. It would be more likely to be 'coded in a form such as 6809430217' where 17 'says which of various possible operations is to be performed on the two numbers'. But how does the machine ensure that the operations are carried out as required? This job falls to a third part of the machine which is neither the 'store' nor the 'executive unit': it is called the 'control'. The duty of the control is 'to see that these

---

[12] Turing, op. cit., p.9.

instructions are obeyed correctly and in the right order'. How does it manage that? Turing's answer is brief and blunt: 'The control is so constructed that this necessarily happens'.[13]

Turing's argument is that intelligence is to be judged by what an agent (human or mechanical) can do, and that as regards the manipulation of symbols a computer has in principle all the resources that a human being has, or their equivalents. So the question of intelligence, as far as its linguistic manifestations are concerned, is simply whether or not in practice a machine can manipulate linguistic symbols with a versatility and effectiveness which match those of a human being. Turing, it must be borne in mind, is describing computers of a kind which were operative in the 1940s. Since those days computers have become much more advanced. Nevertheless, Turing's account is of absorbing interest in retrospect. It documents the way the relationship between minds and machines was being thought of, at least by the academic *avant-garde*, at a time when linguistics was barely emerging from the chrysalis of pre-war structuralism. The intellectual environment which Turing's paper reflects was to have a lasting influence not only on linguistic theorising but also on modern psychology. The connexion with Swift's Balnibarbian language project is self-evident. What Turing announces, in effect, is that the problem originally posed by the grand academy of Lagado is actually soluble, given the right machine. In one respect, the story of the language machine since Swift's day is the story of the progress that has been made towards putting a Balnibarbian Professor of Glottomechanics in a position to build that machine.

Turing's 1950 paper, it should be emphasised, is not concerned with speculation about how the mind might perhaps work, but with description of how existing machines actually did work. The tripartite structure Turing mentions is not a hypothesis, but a fact. What is significant for our present purposes is the metaphorical direction Turing's account takes: he does not try to explain human computation in terms of mechanical computation, but the reverse. His vocabulary humanises the mechanical instead of mechanising the human: *store, control, information, duty,* etc. This is not just a lexical quirk peculiar to Turing, as a glance through a present-day

[13] Turing, op. cit., p.8.

dictionary of computer terminology will confirm.

The vocabulary of modern computation draws extensively on human psychological vocabulary (*checking, selecting, scanning, monitoring*), social vocabulary (*transaction, address, ownership*), and even quasi-political vocabulary (*lock-out, closed shop*). But no source has been more prolific than the vocabulary drawn from language-based activities (*document, statement, record, message, narrative, declaration, notation* and *translation*, to mention only a few). In all these cases, the direction of metaphor is the same as Turing's: the terms make sense by referring the mechanical to the human.

However, it seems clear that, if Turing is right, that metaphorical direction runs counter to the ultimate direction of explanation, which is just the opposite. In other words, many activities traditionally regarded as characteristically human, and hence mechanically inexplicable, will turn out to be at bottom mechanical after all. The idea that this might be true of language is what provides the connecting link with Orwell's prophetic sociology. If what a computer can 'think' is limited by its language, the same may be true of a human being. Hence the notion that a totalitarian government, seeking to control freedon of thought, might achieve that end by standardising a language which promulgates its ideology. If the basic premisses of that ideology can be written into the rules of Newspeak, and Newspeak is the only language, then insofar as systematic thought is impossible without language, the rules of Newspeak will automatically impose the desired restriction on thought.

In short, it is not the technological advances between Swift's day and our own which in themselves explain the promotion of the language machine from a satirical absurdity into an article of scientific faith. What underlies that promotion is a profound change in both lay and academic assumptions concerning the individual's role in the complex of activities we call 'language'. It is here that we must look if we wish to understand how an idea which began as Swift's joke ended up as Orwell's nightmare.

Part I
The Machine Within

For seeing life is but a motion of Limbs, the beginning whereof is in some principall part within; why may we not say, that all Automata (Engines that move themselves by springs and wheels as doth a watch) have an artificiall life?

Hobbes

Chapter One
A Really Loud Voice

The myth of the language machine has a complex history, in which it is possible nevertheless to distinguish certain more or less clearly defined but partially overlapping stages. The earliest and longest of these might be called the 'Galeno-Cartesian' phase. Here, although we find no serious consideration of the extent to which machines might be able to handle language (and if contemplated at all the idea is rapidly dismissed as fantastic or ludicrous, as in *Gulliver's Travels*), for various reasons the complementary question of the extent to which speech in human beings functions 'mechanically' does come up for discussion.

The hypothesis that a special part or parts of the brain control the functions associated with language was already familiar to the Greeks. In the second century AD, Galen believed that experimental interference with a mechanism in the brain could affect vocalisation: he recommended using a pig or a goat instead of an ape for cerebral vivisection, 'because you need an animal with a "really loud voice".'[1] Presumably, therefore, since he treated animal vivisection as a practicable alternative to human vivisection, Galen supposed that all the way down the biological scale, from human being to ape to pig, if not further still, there was a department of the brain which controlled 'speech' (or its equivalent in lower species). This assumption, however, seems to have remained clinically unexplored in antiquity. Not even Herophilus or Erasistratus, although credited with gruesome experiments on Egyptian criminals, anticipated modern science by sticking needles into the living cortex.

Tempting as it is to read back into Graeco-Roman times a recognition of those distinctions which the twentieth century

---

[1] G.E.R.Lloyd, *Science and Morality in Greco-Roman Antiquity*, Cambridge 1985, p.7.

treats as fundamental to the self-understanding of *homo sapiens*, Galen's assumption (if for the argument's sake we can agree to call it that) presents a number of problems. Galen was familiar with the ancient belief, eloquently expressed by Isocrates,[2] that the great divide between living creatures was that only one among them (viz. the human being) had *logos*. The rest did not have *logos*; nor were they capable of achieving it. The normal manifestation of *logos*, however, was in human vocal activity. Speech communication is vocal communication. So where does that leave other animals endowed by nature with a 'really loud voice'? Could it be simply frivolous mimicry on Nature's part to have designed animals with the necessary vocal apparatus, but no *logos* to power it? Galen evidently regarded apes as 'ridiculous imitations' of men,[3] but quite what the cosmic joke is of producing creatures which are ridiculous imitations of others it is difficult to see. The question continued to bemuse philosophers for centuries. Locke pointed out that 'parrots, and several other birds, will be taught to make articulate sounds distinct enough, which yet by no means are capable of language'[4] but could not explain why parrots should have been endowed with such remarkable and utterly pointless skills.

Galen's assumption likewise raises the question of exactly how in human beings voice is related to *logos*. The issue was still being debated in the nineteenth century. Whitney, for instance, held that among the possible modes of expression

> it is simply by a kind of process of natural selection and survival of the fittest that the voice has gained the upper hand, and come to be so much the most prominent that we give the name of *language* ('tonguiness') to all expression. There is no mysterious connection between the thinking apparatus and the articulating apparatus, whereby the action that forms a thought sets the tongue swinging to utter it.[5]

Elsewhere, Whitney claims that in order to explain why the normal and universal mode of human communication is vocal communication, 'it is sufficient to point out the superior

[2] R.Harris, *The Language-Makers*, London 1980, p.168.
[3] Lloyd, loc. cit.
[4] *Essay Concerning Human Understanding*, Bk III, Ch.1.
[5] W.D.Whitney, *The Life and Growth of Language*, 2nd ed., London 1880, p.291.

convenience and availability of spoken signs, as compared with those of any other kind'.[6] Saussure rejected Whitney's view of an absolute separation between the 'thinking apparatus' and the 'articulating apparatus' as too extreme, and advanced the more moderate, albeit extremely vague proposition, that the role of vocalisation as the medium of linguistic expression was 'in some measure imposed upon us by Nature'.[7] But he failed to inquire any further into the nature of that 'imposition'.

Had Galen himself supposed that *logos* was controlled by a quite separate brain mechanism from that controlling voice, it would have been quite pointless performing vivisections on animals in order to investigate the *logos* mechanism, since animals presumably had no such mechanism (unless by chance Nature had indulged in more 'ridiculous imitation', providing even apes and pigs with the mechanism, but playing the ultimate prank on them of disconnecting it from the rest of the brain). The other possibility for Galen to consider would have been simply the possibility that the brain had no *logos* mechanism, either in humans or in animals: that is to say, that the exercise of *logos* was not a physiological activity at all. This would have been to anticipate the view expressed by Descartes in the *Discours de la méthode*: that even if there were machines physically indistinguishable from human bodies, it would always be possible to tell the difference, because of the linguistic limitations of the machines.

> For we can conceive of a machine so constructed that it utters words, and even utters words which correspond to bodily actions causing a change in its organs (e.g. if you touch it in one spot it asks what you want of it, if you touch it in another it cries out that you are hurting it, and so on). But it is not conceivable that such a machine should produce different arrangements of words so as to give an appropriately meaningful answer to whatever is said in its presence, as the dullest of men can do.[8]

Here in Descartes we find the source of Turing's much debated proposal three centuries later that a question-and-answer test

[6] W.D.Whitney, *Language and the Study of Language*, 3rd ed., London 1870, p.421.

[7] F.de Saussure, *Cours de linguistique générale*, 2nd ed., Paris 1922, p.26.

[8] *The Philosophical Writings of Descartes*, tr. J.Cottingham, R.Stoothoff and D.Murdoch, Cambridge 1985, vol.I, p.140.

would suffice to determine whether or not machines can think. In this test, the machine on trial has to take part in what Turing calls the 'imitation game'.

> It is played with three people, a man (A), a woman (B), and an interrogator (C) who may be of either sex. The interrogator stays in a room apart from the other two. The object of the game for the interrogator is to determine which of the other two is the man and which is the woman. He knows them by the labels X and Y, and at the end of the game he says either 'X is A and Y is B' or 'X is B and Y is A'. The interrogator is allowed to put questions to A and B thus:
>
> C: Will X please tell me the length of his or her hair?
>
> Now suppose X is actually A, then A must answer. It is A's object in the game to try to cause C to make the wrong identification. His answer might therefore be
>
> 'My hair is shingled, and the longest strands are about nine inches long.'
>
> In order that tones of voice may not help the interrogator the answers should be written, or better still, typewritten. The ideal arrangement is to have a teleprinter communicating between the two rooms. Alternatively the questions and answers can be repeated by an intermediary. The object of the game for the third player (B) is to help the interrogator. The best strategy for her is to give truthful answers. She can add such things as 'I am the woman, don't listen to him!' to her answers, but it will avail nothing as the man can make similar remarks.
>
> We now ask the question, 'What will happen when a machine takes the part of A in this game?' Will the interrogator decide wrongly as often when the game is played like this as he does when the game is played between a man and a woman? These questions replace our original, 'Can machines think?'[9]

Turing's originality in devising this test is the originality of having taken Descartes' argument at face value and squared up to its challenge. Turing assumes, in other words, that if a machine can be built which passes the test of the 'imitation game', that will constitute an empirical disproof of Descartes' thesis. For in order to pass the test, Turing clearly assumes that the machine must possess a *linguistic* capacity: that of analysing the interrogator's questions and returning appropriate answers.

Whether Descartes originally intended the 'language machine' argument to be taken literally is another question. It is bound up

---

[9] Turing, op. cit., p.5.

with the more basic question of whether for Descartes *la bête machine* is a genuine physiological hypothesis or merely a metaphor. To judge by the evidence of the *Discours de la méthode*, the balance is a delicate one. The process by which originally metaphorical descriptions are subsequently shown, by 'ontological experiment', to constitute accurate factual accounts of how Nature works is sometimes said to be characteristic of progress in the natural sciences.[10] But undoubtedly Descartes would have denied that any machine built by Turing, or by Turing's imagination, could produce answers to satisfy or confuse the interrogator in the 'imitation game'. Descartes, in short, would have refused to accept the imitation game as a legitimate 'ontological experiment': not because of any technical flaw in the experimental design, but because from a Cartesian point of view the question is already begged once the teleprinter text produced by the machine in the next room is construed as an 'answer' to the interrogator.

Nor would Descartes have been impressed by an animal responding to Turing's interrogator in 'a really loud voice'. It is not

> because they lack the necessary organs, for we see that magpies and parrots can utter words as we do, and yet they cannot speak as we do: that is, they cannot show that they are thinking what they are saying. On the other hand, men born deaf and dumb, and thus deprived of speech-organs as much as the beasts or even more so, normally invent their own signs to make themselves understood by those who, being regularly in their company, have the time to learn their language. This shows not merely that the beasts have less reason than men, but that they have no reason at all. For it patently requires very little reason to be able to speak.[11]

In the centuries following, this argument was echoed by many writers who would not necessarily have agreed entirely with Descartes that there is simply no connexion between having a voice and having *logos*, and no question of interaction between two specialised cerebral mechanisms. For Descartes, the human brain is part of the human body, and the body is a machine. 'The whole nature of the body consists in its being an extended thing; and there is absolutely nothing in common between thought and

[10] R.Harré, *Theories and Things*, London 1961.
[11] Descartes, loc. cit.

extension.'[12] *Logos*, in short, unlike voice, has no mechanical apparatus of its own at all. Hence the fact that animals lack *logos* is in no way attributable to a merely physiological deficiency.

Two points about Descartes' position on animal behaviour are worth emphasising in the present context. The first is its connexion with the traditional Western assumption that linguistic communication involves a process of telementation.[13] In effect, Descartes presents a more rigorous and intransigent formulation of the telementational doctrine than any of his predecessors. He is highly critical of compromises (such as Montaigne's[14]) which would attribute to animals a lesser form of telementation, based on the supposition that animals might have 'languages' which human beings simply do not understand. For Descartes, whatever form animal communication may take it cannot constitute *linguistic* communication because animals do not have minds, and consequently have no thoughts which could possibly be the subject of telementational transference from one member of the species to another. To maintain this, clearly, is to take telementation to be not merely the *normal function* of linguistic communication but a *necessary condition* of linguistic communication; and an immediate corollary is that no communication system which is not used for telementation counts as a language. This dogmatic Cartesian distinction between language and other modes of communication survives into the twentieth century in some surprising theoretical guises. It underlies, for example, psychological theories of children's language acquisition such as Vygotsky's, which assumes that up to a certain stage in the child's development 'thought' and 'speech' are independent, and that 'true' language is acquired at the nexal point when 'thought becomes verbal and speech rational'.[15]

The second point is that insofar as talking involves the same kind of vocal-auditory processes that are found in animals, there must be a component of human speech behaviour which is to be accounted for in purely mechanical terms, in just the same way

---

[12] Descartes, op. cit., vol.II, p.248.

[13] R.Harris, *The Language Myth*, London 1980.

[14] A.Robinet, *Le langage à l'âge classique*, Paris 1978, p.95ff.

[15] L.S.Vygotsky, *Thought and Language*, 1934: English tr. Cambridge, Mass. 1962, p.44.

as all other physiological phenomena. To put Descartes' view in a Galenian perspective, we might say that there must be a human *speech* mechanism (or mechanisms) which cerebral vivisection could in principle discover, but there could not be a *language* mechanism. So if Galen thought that vivisection, whether of humans, pigs or apes, could discover anything about language he was, from Descartes' point of view, guilty of a conceptual confusion.

The extent to which the Cartesian concept of *la bête machine* continues to dominate the twentieth-century study of animal communication is remarkable. It reveals itself in many ways. Perhaps the most obvious is the extreme diffidence, even reluctance, with which ethologists in their descriptions of animal behaviour attribute intentionality to animals or meanings to the signals animals use in their natural environment. There are still those who 'see the intentional, mentalist account as appropriate only to humans, denying that this mode is ever acceptable or scientific or true as regards nonhuman animals' and many more who 'see the intentional, mentalist account as appropriate only to organisms that have language'.[16]

The two main reasons nowadays given for refusing to assimilate the meaning of animal signals to the meaning of human linguistic signals are both essentially Cartesian reasons. One is that animal signals are characteristically 'stimulus-bound', and the other is that most animal signals are restricted to communicating one of a limited, non-productive set of fixed messages known to all members of the species. The meaning of a linguistic signal, by contrast, is alleged to be typically free from stimulus control, and is not necessarily drawn from a set of messages known in advance to all human beings. The nearest human equivalents to animal signalling are regarded as being certain forms of spontaneous, involuntary expression, such as blushing, weeping, inarticulate exclamations of pain, etc. Although these forms of expression are in one sense communicative, they are held to be of an entirely different nature from linguistic communication. This idea, again, can be traced back to the *Discours de la méthode*, which explicitly warns us that 'we must not confuse speech with the natural movements

---

[16] J.Leiber, 'The strange creature', *The Meaning of Primate Signals*, ed. R.Harré and V.Reynolds, Cambridge 1984, p.77.

which express passions and which can be imitated by machines as well as animals'.[17]

The spectre of *la bête machine* also raises its head in arguments about the success or failure of programmes to teach primates sign language. Descartes would have been no more impressed by the progress of Washoe, Sarah and their peers than latter-day sceptics like H.S.Terrace.[18] As we know from his correspondence,[19] Descartes thought that the reason why it was possible to train a magpie to say 'bonjour' was not that the bird could be brought to understand the meaning of the word but that its utterance could, with suitable conditioning, become the expression of one of the bird's natural desires: for instance, the desire for food. Similarly nowadays the standard objection to glossing the fact that a monkey learns to use a specific gesture systematically in trainer interactions to elicit the reward of a banana as 'the monkey knows that this sign means "banana"' is that this constitutes an overinterpretation of the evidence. The validity of the gloss is denied on the ground that all that has been shown is that the monkey likes bananas and has found a reliable way of getting them. This, it is argued, fails to demonstrate that the monkey knows the sign has any meaning at all, let alone the specific meaning 'banana'. Clearly, debates of this kind would be pointless unless it were assumed that on the legitimacy of the meaning-ascription hangs some deep issue as to whether or not the animal's behaviour is 'merely mechanical'. Descartes would also have dismissed the objection that from his own explanation of the magpie's performance it emerges that the magpie is at least capable of learning a sign for 'food' (even if, as it happens, this is not the correct meaning of *bonjour*): for, as noted above, Descartes denies that 'movements which express passions' are signs at all in the relevant sense. In short, as far as animals were concerned, Descartes was already a committed behaviourist *avant la lettre*.

It should be noted, however, that Descartes can hardly be held to blame for a particularly crass variety of *bête machine* argument occasionally encountered nowadays. This attempts to

[17] Descartes, op. cit., vol.I, pp.140-1.
[18] H.S.Terrace,' "Language" in apes', *The Meaning of Primate Signals*, ed. R.Harré and V.Reynolds, Cambridge 1984; *Nim*, New York 1979.
[19] R.Descartes, *Discours de la méthode*, ed. E.Gilson, 5th ed., Paris 1976, p.428.

prove that animal communication is 'merely mechanical' by the simple expedient of demonstrating that it breaks down when interfered with. A blatant example is the argument adduced by Fromkin and Rodman[20] to show that the dance communication by honeybees of messages about the location of sources of nectar is not *linguistic* communication. The evidence they cite comes from a curious experiment in which, instead of being allowed to fly to the source of nectar, a bee was made to walk. Upon returning to the hive from this experience unprecedented in apian history, the ambulatory bee attempted to communicate the whereabouts of the nectar to its fellows, but woefully misinformed them, having overestimated the distance of the nectar by a factor of 25. This shows, claim Fromkin and Rodman, that the bee when forced to walk 'had no way of communicating the special circumstances or taking them into account in its message. This absence of *creativity* makes the bee's dance qualitatively different from human language.'

The argument is arrestingly bizarre. It is on a par with claiming that if we blindfold Smith and discover that he can no longer make reliable judgements about which direction is north and which south, that proves Smith's earlier correct statements 'this direction is north' and 'this direction is south' were not acts of linguistic communication at all. That the ambulatory bee got the distance hopelessly wrong, as a result – presumably – of being deprived of the cues bees normally rely on, says nothing at all about the status of the bees' communication system as a language. Even more bizarre is the implication that if Nature had providently equipped the honeybee with a dance which allowed it to distinguish between distances calculated on the basis of flying, walking, and other modes of locomotion, however improbable in a bee's life, that fact would count in favour of recognising the dance signs as genuine linguistic signs. The underlying idea here seems to be that 'creativity' in communication (which the bee's dance allegedly lacks) is a matter of adaptability to totally unforeseeable eventualities. This is what provides the link with Descartes' notion that a machine (and for Descartes a bee could be nothing more) would be incapable of producing an appropriately meaningful response

[20] V.Fromkin and R.Rodman, *An Introduction to Language*, 2nd ed., New York 1978, p.42.

in all circumstances. But Descartes would never have made the grotesque blunder of trying to press this claim on the basis of experiments designed to confuse the normal behaviour patterns of unsuspecting animals. For then the argument immediately courts self-defeat, since *no* communication system is foolproof against *all* possibilities (where *all* possibilities include the possibility that the system itself is based on assumptions which no longer hold). If that were the requirement, then English, French, Latin or any other language would fail to meet it, just as the bees' communication system does; and therefore it would be futile to take the appropriate use of language as the yardstick of rationality.

In order to make sense of Descartes' criterion we have to exclude any demand that communication systems be adaptable to circumstances which make their normal functioning impossible. To take a simple example, our numerical vocabulary is suited to situations in which a certain stability in the properties of physical objects is guaranteed. That vocabulary could not be instantly adapted to a world in which things were constantly and randomly changing their size, shape and number; for in such an unstable world the application of our familiar quantificational concepts finds no place. As a famous mathematician once observed about the miracle of the Council of Nicaea, there is no possibility of counting bishops who keep exchanging corporeal identities with one another.[21] It is not that a special 'Nicaean mathematics' would be needed; but rather that Nicaean situations fall outside mathematics altogether.

The point is of some importance since Descartes' linguistic criterion for distinguishing between human beings and machines becomes meaningless once we start envisaging communication situations which are quite beyond the capacity of the communication system. To put the same point slightly differently, there is no universal Turing test valid science-fictionally across 'all possible worlds'. The reason for this is simply that it soon becomes radically unclear by what criteria the answers to Turing-test questions are to be judged appropriate or inappropriate once the basic assumptions of our familiar everyday world are abandoned or suspended. The

---

[21] A.N.Whitehead, 'Mathematics', *Encyclopaedia Britannica*, 11th ed., vol.17, Cambridge 1911, p.881.

further we venture from those basic assumptions the more difficult it will become to distinguish reliably between 'intelligent' responses and 'unintelligent' ones; or indeed between intelligible responses and unintelligible ones. All Descartes seems to have had in mind was that it is quite easy to detect a speaking automaton, however cunningly disguised as a human, by asking it a straightforward question it has not been programmed to answer ('What day of the week is it?', 'What colour is grass?', 'What do you use a knife for?', etc.). The assumption, clearly, is that automata cannot be built which provide appropriate answers to a general range of such questions. But what becomes of Descartes' criterion if advances in technology prove that assumption unsound? Turing's answer is plain enough: we then have to stop claiming that machines (or monkeys, if monkeys can be trained to pass the Turing test) cannot think.

Turing's position is in all essentials a radical behaviourist position, which treats 'thinking' as being simply speech minus vocalisation.[22] The only evidence that the Turing test accepts or requires about thought is verbal evidence. The implication is that provided this verbal evidence convinces the human investigator as being appropriate to the questions asked, there is nothing more that can be demanded as evidence of thinking. Turing's behaviourist strategy of taking Descartes' language-machine argument seriously thus stands the traditional view of language on its head. The irony is that Descartes himself had opened the way for this move by so strenuously denying any connexion between having reason and having a voice. His assimilation of animals to machines, his acknowledgement that animals can vocalise, and his insistence on language as the hallmark of rationality jointly obliged Descartes to distinguish sharply in human speech between a mechanical and a non-mechanical component. The legacy of that dualism survived into nineteenth-century linguistics, which still accepted a distinction between purely mechanical, physiological processes (as evidenced in phonology) and non-mechanical 'intellectual' processes (as evidenced in semantics and the workings of analogy). However, the Cartesian concept of *la bête machine* had already prepared the ground for the anti-Cartesian concept of

[22] Harris, op. cit. p.159f.

l'homme machine.[23] Given the theory of *l'homme machine,*
Descartes' mysterious non-mechanical component of human
speech had in the end either to be dismissed as a mere figment of
Cartesian mentalism, or else reinterpreted by reference to a
second cerebral mechanism, distinct from but interacting with
the mechanism of vocalisation. By the end of the nineteenth
century, many people – including many linguists – believed that
the exact location of this second mechanism in the brain had at
last been identified. Thus in spite of the fact that Descartes was
a committed anti-mechanist where language was concerned, the
Cartesian contribution to the modern myth of the language
machine is in its way no less crucial than the contribution which
was to be made by Saussure. For Saussure, however, the
distribution of 'mechanical' explanations is almost the opposite
of Descartes': it was to be *parole* over which individuals could
exercise rational control in the Cartesian sense, whereas over
langue they had none.

[23] L.C.Rosenfield, *From Beast-Machine to Man-Machine*, New York 1941.

Chapter Two

The Gutenberg Connexion

An essential link between linguistics in Lagado and linguistics in Oceania is linguistics in Geneva. There in 1916 the publication of Saussure's *Cours de linguistique générale* announced a charter for linguistic inquiry in which we find for the first time an extended and serious development of the idea of a linguistic 'mechanism'. Without bringing Saussure into the picture, we are unlikely to appreciate that 'Why is the grand academy's language automation project ridiculous?' is both a more difficult and a more rewarding question than at first sight may appear. The potential reward is enhanced once it is realised that what we are asking is a question concerning one of the most important episodes in the post-Renaissance history of Western ideas about *homo loquens* as language-maker. But the potential difficulty is increased once it is realised that the answers Swift's contemporaries might have given are not necessarily those we would give today.

What in all probability strikes the late-twentieth-century reader as so absurd about the project which Gulliver inspected is not the idea of the mechanisation of linguistic skills as such – far from it – but the fact that to construct a machine like the language frame of Lagado is to set about the problem of mechanisation in entirely the wrong way. The theory behind the language frame nowadays appears unscientific, and for a quite specific reason: it fails to come to terms with the truth that linguistic texts are not produced by random processes, but in accordance with rules. Provided the Professor of Glotto-mechanics has grasped that fundamental principle, we see no reason why he should not at least make some progress towards the goal of designing his Balnibarbian language machine.

That is in part because our generation has already assimilated certain lessons in linguistics from Geneva: the chapter of

37

Saussure's *Cours* entitled 'Mécanisme de la langue' represents
the language-user as the operator of a mental device which offers
a series of choices. It is Saussure who gives the first detailed
description of how this psycholinguistic machinery works. What
is remarkable is that the possibilities of choice are articulated in
just two dimensions, precisely as in the 'wonderful machine'
which Gulliver inspected in Lagado. Saussure called the two
dimensions 'associative' and 'syntagmatic'. Later Saussureans
called them 'paradigmatic' and 'syntagmatic'. What they were
called in Balnibarbian Swift does not tell us: but they correspond
respectively (i) to the choices presented on the various facets of
each revolving piece of wood in the 'wonderful machine', and (ii)
to the choices presented by the possibilities of linear alignment
of the pieces along any particular wire in the frame.

These choices interlock, both in Swift's version and in
Saussure's. In other words, the relations between

> *I went home*
> *You went home*
> *He went home*
> *She went home*
> *We went home*
> *They went home*

are construed as corresponding to opting for various possibilities
in filling the first slot in an otherwise identical linear
syntagmatic structure. At the same time, these various
'horizontal' structures are construed as possible concatenations
of units chosen by opting between various 'vertical' possibilities.
Thus each of the above syntagmas represents a multiple
associative choice. *I went home* is chosen from among

> *I came home*
> *I ran home*
> *I walked home*
> *I drove home*
> ...etc.

and, at the same time, from among

> *I went out*

I went back
I went in
I went away
...etc.

This Saussurean two-dimensional analysis is manifestly a generalisation from the machinery Gulliver inspected in Lagado. The generalisation proceeds by assuming (i) that the wires in the frame may be of variable length, and (ii) that the blocks of wood strung along each wire may have a variable number of facets.

The importance of Saussure's role in the story of the language machine hinges on the two facts: (i) that he was the first linguist to insist that linguistics could not be a science unless it proposed a method of linguistic analysis corresponding to real processes in the mind of the ordinary language-user, and (ii) that he treated his account of the 'language mechanism' not as a fanciful metaphor or abstraction, but as a description – in outline at least – of those psycholinguistic processes. The modern belief that there must be a real – and not just a figurative – language machine in the mind owes an ineradicable debt to Saussure. But Saussure's contribution has to be evaluated against the background of the discoveries about the human brain which had been made only a generation previously by Broca.

Broca can easily be seen retrospectively, if we wish to see him thus, as a latter-day phrenologist. The term *phrenology* is nowadays so commonly used dismissively as the designation of a long-discredited pseudo-science that it is perhaps worth quoting what were taken as being its essential doctrines when it was still taken 'seriously'. They were, according to one source,[1] five in number:

(1) the brain is the organ of the mind; (2) the mental powers of man can be analysed into a definite number of independent faculties; (3) these faculties are innate, and each has its seat in a definite region of the brain; (4) the size of each such region is the measure of the degree to which the faculty seated in it forms a constituent element in the character of the individual; (5) the correspondence between the outer surface of the skull and the contour of the brain surface beneath is sufficiently close to enable

[1] A.Macalister, 'Phrenology', *Encyclopaedia Britannica*, 11th ed., vol.21, Cambridge 1911, p.534.

the observer to recognize the relative sizes of these several organs by the examination of the outer surface of the head.

The popular notion of phrenology seizes upon doctrine (5) and supposes that an individual's mental make-up can be 'read' by feeling bumps on the head: at which point phrenology is reduced to a kind of cranial version of palmistry. But this is merely an inessential appendage to the central phrenological thesis, which is nowadays described non-dismissively as 'localisation theory'.

Ever since Flourens' criticisms of Gall, 'localisation theory' had been the subject of debate. 'In its extreme form, the theory states that there is a strict one-to-one relationship between the anatomical areas of the brain and bodily function.'[2] Although Broca himself did not advance the 'extreme form' of localisation theory, in the 1860s he had reported 'a finding whose importance for subsequent scientific inquiry is difficult to overestimate';[3] namely, that in the cases of two aphasic patients, loss of language was associated with damage to quite specific sites in the brain. Subsequent work in aphasiology by Wernicke and Déjerine was generally taken as providing support for the view that Broca's claims were, in outline if not necessarily in detail, along the right lines.

Broca's nineteenth-century clinical investigations of brain damage in linguistically handicapped patients are here of significance not so much for what Broca actually discovered as for what linguists understood Broca to have discovered. What they understood Broca to have discovered is not in doubt, for it is revealed by their own explicit testimony. Already in the 1870's Broca's work was having an influence in European linguistics, and in France we find mention of it even in an introductory manual like Abel Hovelacque's *La linguistique*,[4] designed for students following the established curricula of comparative philology.

Broca is credited with having shown that 'we speak with the left hemisphere'; that being where the *faculté du langage articulé* is usually localised, in a specific part of the third frontal convolution. Broca's explanation for this is given as being that the infant normally has to embark on the difficult task of

---

[2] D.Crystal, *Introduction to Language Pathology*, London 1980, p.90.
[3] H.Gardner, *The Mind's New Science*, New York 1985, p.267.
[4] 2nd ed., Paris 1877.

language acquisition at a stage when the development of the left hemisphere is more advanced than that of the right hemisphere, and consequently better able to 'direct the execution and co-ordination of those acts, which are at one and the same time intellectual and muscular, which constitute articulated language'.[5] (The notion of an act which is both 'intellectual and muscular' we may note in passing as one of particular interest in the present context.)

Hovelacque also quotes Broca on the distinction between a *faculté générale du langage* and a *faculté spéciale du langage articulé*. The function of the former is to 'establish a determinate relationship between an idea and a sign', while the more specialised function of the latter is to establish 'a relationship between an idea and an articulated word'. A further distinction drawn by Broca is between the faculty of expression and the faculty of connexion. This is held to correspond to a difference of brain localisation, on the basis of the following argument: a severe lesion of the left hemisphere may deprive the patient of the ability to utter speech, but leave intact the ability to understand speech, thus indicating on the one hand that the right hemisphere can take over the work of maintaining connexions between ideas and words, but on the other hand that it cannot take over the work of expressing these connexions by the co-ordinated movements demanded for utterance.

Broca is cited by Hovelacque as insisting that the site of articulated language is not the muscles, nor the motor nerves, nor the cerebral motor organs, since these can exist perfectly formed and undamaged 'in individuals who have become entirely aphemic or in idiots who have never been able to learn or understand any kind of language at all'. Broca's doctrine of localisation, claims Hovelacque, has been amply confirmed by all the available medical evidence, and he takes this as establishing beyond any doubt that linguistics (as distinct from philology) belongs to the natural sciences.[6] Broca thus plays a key part for linguists in rejecting the old identification of the language 'mechanism' with the workings of the vocal apparatus (as commonly found in the eighteenth century, for example in de Brosses' *Traité de la formation méchanique des langues*, and

[5] Hovelacque, op. cit., p.32.
[6] ibid., p.34.

exemplified only too clearly in both medical and social practice by the treatment accorded to the dumb.)

Now Hovelacque's book would have been in all likelihood already familiar to Saussure in his student days. If so, it is all the more interesting to compare what Saussure made of Broca's discoveries with what Hovelacque says about them. In Saussure's *Cours* there is just a single reference to Broca, but it is a very crucial one in Saussure's argument concerning the scope of linguistics. Unlike Hovelacque, Saussure does not draw the conclusion that linguistics belongs to the natural sciences. The *Cours* says,

> Broca discovered that the faculty of speech is localised in the third frontal convolution of the left hemisphere of the brain. This fact has been seized upon to justify regarding language as a natural endowment. But the same localisation is known to hold for *everything* connected with language, including writing. Thus what seems to be indicated when we take into consideration also the evidence from various forms of aphasia due to lesions in the centres of localisation is: (1) that the various disorders which affect spoken language are interconnected in many ways with disorders affecting written language, and (2) that in all cases of aphasia or agraphia what is affected is not so much the ability to utter or inscribe this or that, but the ability to produce in any given mode signs corresponding to normal language. All this leads us to believe that, over and above the functioning of the various organs, there exists a more general faculty governing signs, which may be regarded as the linguistic faculty *par excellence*.[7]

This puts quite a different slant on the evidence from brain damage. Although Saussure is more than willing to accept Broca's postulation of a general human sign faculty which is 'the linguistic faculty *par excellence*', he is careful not to draw attention to Broca's explicit distinctions between the 'general' and the 'special' linguistic faculties. This is because Saussure is keen to deny that there is any (e.g. neuro-anatomical) basis for establishing linguistics as a science, *other than* the social recognition of languages as communication systems. In effect, this means that Saussure simply ignores what for Broca is 'special' about *le langage articulé*. It also suits Saussure's book to accept with Broca the notion that language is basically a matter of one-one correlations between signs (or words) and ideas in the

[7] Saussure, op. cit., pp.26-7.

brain. He does not quarrel with Broca's apparent assumption that 'ideas' can be treated for neurolinguistic purposes as a single undifferentiated category, since this fits in with his own bi-planar analysis of the linguistic sign; nor with Broca's assumption that neurolinguistic organisation is based on minimal significant units of some kind. At the same time, however, he ignores Broca's argument for recognising a physiological difference between a linguistic faculty of expression and a linguistic faculty of connexion. For Saussure, the connexions have to be presented as a systematic core of *langage articulé* (i.e. *langue*), whereas everything else has to be relegated to *parole*. All this, to say the least, involves a considerable oversimplification by Saussure of the clinical picture then in the process of emerging, if not a crude distortion.

What Saussure the linguist could not afford to do (much as he obviously would have liked to) was simply to ignore Broca the physiologist. That would have left Saussurean linguistics vulnerable to the charge of failing to take cognisance of the latest scientific investigations bearing upon its proclaimed subject of inquiry. Jakobson's later interpretation of the evidence from aphasia[8] is a classically Saussurean manoeuvre of the same stamp. In short, modern linguistic theory recognised at quite an early stage that its academic credibility depended on paying lip-service to research in the natural sciences which seemed to bear directly upon the human language faculty, while at the same time continuing to make the world safe for linguists to pursue their traditional lines of inquiry unhindered.

It now seems ironical that Saussure's great achievement should be regarded as the 'internalisation' of the object of study in linguistics.[9] In fact it was the growing importance of aphasiology in the 1860s and 1870s which forced linguists to face a potential schism in their subject. Linguistics either had to abandon its claim to be the 'science of language', or else, as Hovelacque saw, had to face up to the obligations incumbent upon joining the ranks of the natural sciences. This would mean switching attention away from predominantly historical preoccupations with the development and diversification of language families, and concentrating instead on the experimental investigation of language

[8] See below, p.56ff.
[9] Harris, op. cit., p.47 ff.

as a cognitive system in the individual (a task for which the young linguists of Saussure's generation lacked both scientific training and – as far as one can tell in retrospect – any inclination).

The Saussurean programme for linguistics was an ingenious and face-saving compromise. It turned on the identification of an object of study which could be presented as *both* a cognitive system in the individual *and* a social institution in the community at one and the same time. This object of study was the curious Saussurean abstraction *la langue*, which Saussure was careful to distinguish from *le langage*. Clio's dues were rendered unto Clio by hiving off historical studies under the head of 'diachronic linguistics', and at the same time denying that diachronic phenomena were in any sense part of *la langue*. What was brilliant about Saussure's solution was that aphasiology had so far said nothing about *la langue* in the Saussurean sense, only about *le langage*. Yet, by the aphasiologists' own account, it could be argued to be at the weakest a plausible hypothesis and at the strongest a logical requirement that the normal adult brain's linguistic equipment should somewhere include a systematisation corresponding to *la langue*. That seemed unquestionable if one adopted – as Saussure proceeded to do on behalf of linguistics – a Lockean psychological model of communication.[10]

Locke had been the first thinker in the Western tradition to propose in effect a 'cognitive' definition of the term *language*, and thereby to prise the concept of a language free from its ordinary cultural implications. For if we accept Locke's claim that there are *two* languages in use in every communication situation where speaker and hearer do not associate the same sounds with the same ideas,[11] it follows that what is ordinarily called 'the English language' may in communicational reality subsume indefinitely many different languages, even though speakers of 'English' themselves do not realise that fact. Locke, in short, made invariance of verbally communicated ideas a necessary condition of linguistic identity.

The Lockean model, which Saussure revamped in the form of a *circuit de la parole*, incorporated as the essential requirement of

[10] ibid., Ch.4.
[11] ibid., p.86.

successful communication that the words uttered by the speaker should be decoded in the mind of the hearer to yield exactly the same ideas as originally formulated in the mind of the speaker. In various guises,[12] this basic model of communication has survived in linguistics from the publication of Saussure's *Cours* down to the present day.

Saussure's contribution to the model was twofold. Locke left behind him a 'communicational puzzle'.[13] Saussure solved it. The puzzle resides in what Locke called 'the imperfection of words'. The imperfection is that a word can signify only a thought in the mind of the speaker. Since a hearer has no independent access to the mind of the speaker, the best a hearer can do is to interpret the word as signifying some thought in the hearer's mind. But that yields no guarantee of identity between the speaker's thought and the hearer's thought. Nevertheless, for most everyday purposes it seems that the 'imperfection of words' does not in practice hinder communication. It was not part of Locke's concern to solve this communicational puzzle, but it was taken up by his eighteenth-century successors. Saussure's solution is perhaps the most remarkable in a long line of attempts. Its technique is the effective but brutal technique of cutting Gordian knots. Saussure, in other words, simply defines *la langue* as a system which guarantees to its users the identity between speaker's and hearer's thoughts which Locke leaves as problematic. If the Saussurean hearer does not interpret the word in the same way as the speaker who uttered it, then they are not using the same *langue*.

Saussure's second contribution was to extend the model. Instead of being just an account of how individual ideas are transmitted, it becomes a model applicable to the totality of signalling devices involved in linguistic communication. Speaker and hearer must operate with the same fixed code in all their linguistic dealings with each other, or else at some point communication between them will break down. Saussure, unlike Locke, does not conceive of communication proceeding 'one word at a time', in the sense that the meaning of one word is independent of – and can be understood independently of – the meaning of any other word. Saussure's conception of *langue* is

[12] R.Harris, *Reading Saussure*, London 1987, Part II, Ch.2.

[13] T.J.Taylor, 'Linguistic origins: Bruner and Condillac on learning how to talk', *Language & Communication* 4, 1984.

holistic: no part is isolable from any other part. So speaker and hearer share the whole linguistic code in common – or nothing.

Saussure's version of the model, therefore, has extensive practical implications. In 'real life', the only likelihood that speaker and hearer will have equal access to the same fixed code depends on both having been brought up as – or in maturity becoming – members of the same linguistic community. Saussurean linguistics redefines the linguistic community by reference to *la langue*, instead of treating the communal practice as the basis for defining the community's language. Thus it emerges that instead of brain activity explaining speech, the social institution of a common language becomes a logical prerequisite for explaining what goes on in the 'linguistic section' of the brain.

Saussure's strategy, in brief, is to turn the tables on the major linguistic problem of his generation. Instead of following the lead of the aphasiologists and taking linguistics down the experimental path of the natural sciences, the Saussurean programme simply declares in advance an equation between cognitive system and social institution. Both are *la langue*; or, more precisely, the cognitive system must have as its basis a faithful internalised 'representation' of *la langue*. This being so, it becomes unnecessary for linguistics to concern itself with what goes on in the brain, even while admitting that what goes on in the brain is crucial. For *la langue* is more readily available for inspection by the linguist 'out in the open': that is to say, in the daily social practices which go to make up the speech activity of the community. The totality of this overt activity Saussure subsumes under *parole*. So although in principle there are two possible ways of investigating *la langue*, a neurophysiological route and a social-observation route, the latter is far easier and leads to exactly the same investigatory goal as the former. Linguists need not wear white coats or wield scalpels after all, (which must have brought immediate relief to those who had read about Broca's discoveries with mounting dismay). Linguistics was thereby saved from the ignominy of the autopsy table.

The logic of the Saussurean solution is, unfortunately, deeply flawed. The flaws emerge clearly enough in retrospect from the very strategy adopted in the chapter in the *Cours* on 'Mécanisme de la langue'. Postulation of a cognitive 'mechanism' is forced on Saussure by two requirements, one relating to *langue* and the other to *parole*. Without it, he has no way of describing how in *la langue* syntagmatic relations and associative relations inter-mesh; for each is based, as the *Cours* admits, on a quite different principle of comparison. 'The whole set of phonetic and conceptual differences which constitute *la langue* are ... the product of two kinds of comparison.'[14] Now comparison cannot be other than a cognitive activity. It presupposes the adoption of a *basis* for comparison. But since, as Saussure concedes, syntagmatic and associative comparisons rest on two quite different bases, the problem arises of explaining how, psychologically, it is possible to identify units across the comparative gap. What is the comparative basis for comparing intrinsically disparate comparisons? This is the key psychological question on which the entire plausibility of the Saussurean account of linguistic structure depends.

It is to Saussure's enduring credit that, unlike many linguists before and since his day, he actually recognised this as a problem. He rejected the easy way out, which makes the facile assumption that linguistic units are just 'given' in advance of linguistic activity. Instead, he set himself the task of explaining how such units are 'created' by the mind on the basis of the individual's experience of speech. The mind subjects this experience, according to Saussure, to two types of comparison. One is a comparison based on temporal sequence. This gives rise to the Saussurean dimension of 'linearity'. The other is a comparison based on non-linear criteria: similarities of form, of meaning, or of both combined. Such comparisons, considered globally as an alternative dimension to linearity, are subsumed under 'association'. Associative relations, therefore, are defined negatively with respect to linear relations. That is ultimately why the 'principle of linearity' (and not any alternative 'principle of association') features as one of the two basic Saussurean principles of linguistics, along with the much-disputed 'principle of arbitrariness'.

It thus emerges as essential for Saussure's purposes that there should be no mismatch between the units identified by syntagmatic comparison and the units identified by associative

[14] Saussure, op. cit., p.176.

comparison. Whether the mind engages in one type of comparison or the other must make no difference. Otherwise we might presumably understand utterances differently depending on whether they were analysed on a 'linear' (i.e. syntagmatic) basis, or on a 'non-linear' (i.e. associative) basis. But that would make nonsense of *langue* as an integrated system guaranteeing that both speaker and hearer identify exactly the 'same' messages. Therefore, Saussure is obliged to safeguard his own account of how linguistic communication works by postulating that the third frontal convolution of the left hemisphere (or whatever other cerebral site aphasiologists might identify) operates like 'a machine in which the components all act upon one another, even though they are arranged in one dimension only'.[15] In other words, there is *no* comparative basis for linking syntagmatic with associative units; the linguistic component of the brain is just organised, fortunately for us, in a way which ensures that linkage. Like the 'control' component of Turing's computer, it 'is so constructed that this necessarily happens'. This, then, is the first function of Saussure's *mécanisme de la langue*.

The second function relates to the way *langue* is put to use in *parole*. In Saussure's account, the force of the terms 'mechanism' and 'machine' is precisely that they imply an automatic co-ordination between various parts, requiring no extraneous explanation. This makes it unnecessary for Saussure to call upon any further psychological activity to tackle a basic problem as to how the speaker expresses a thought in the verbally appropriate manner. Once the thought has been selected by the speaker, the machine goes into action. It operates below the level of consciousness. It analyses the thought into its component parts and identifies the appropriate sign for each part.

> Our memory holds in store all the various complex types of syntagma, of every kind and length. When a syntagma is brought into use, we call upon associative groups in order to make our choice. So when someone says *marchons!* ('let's march!') he thinks unconsciously of various associative groups, at whose common intersection appears the syntagma *marchons!* This syntagma belongs to one series which includes the singular imperative *marche!* ('march!') and the 2nd person plural

---

[15] ibid., p.177.

imperative *marchez!* ('march!'), and *marchons!* stands in opposition to both as a form selected from this group. At the same time, it belongs to another series which includes *montons!* ('let's go up!'), *mangeons!* ('let's eat!') etc., and represents a selection from this group as well. In each series, it is known which factor to vary in order to obtain the differentiation appropriate to the unit sought.[16]

In other words, the machinery described by Saussure is designed in just such a way as to eliminate what would otherwise be the mystery of how the appropriate syntagma assembles itself out of an unordered assortment of parts (which is all that the memory's associative groups allegedly provide). This is eliminated because syntagmas like *marchons!* are already stored in the machine as whole units: thus there is no question of the speaker 'deciding' to combine the parts in some other way, or 'not knowing' how they ought to be combined.

This Heath Robinson sketch of how the combinatorial apparatus works fills a rather conspicuous gap left in Saussure's *circuit de la parole*. There the reader was rather cryptically informed that concepts 'trigger' acoustic images, but no explanation was given of how the triggering process could result in the formation of any complex structure. To that extent, it may be said that Saussure's *mécanisme de la langue* performs adequately the only functions it was ever intended to perform. But considered on its own merits as a theory of the cognitive workings of the linguistic system, it is highly unsatisfactory. For it merely projects hypothetically into the cerebral cortex a prefabricated contrivance designed to handle traditional morphological units. By postulating that this contrivance produces the desired syntagma automatically, Saussure does not answer – but rather evades – the question of how language is organised in the brain.

Nowhere does the *Cours* explain why it should follow that, because *marchons!* is traditionally analysed into a stem and a flexion, each of which it shares with other forms, we are entitled to assume without further ado that the storage system in the brain simply comprises lists of such forms, based on common components, and that selecting *marchons!* involves matching the items on two (or more) such lists. Many other storage

[16] ibid., p.179.

systems are in theory feasible. All that is clear is that Saussure does not wish to entertain, for example, the possibility that stems and flexions are stored separately; since that would immediately give rise to a syntagmatic assembly problem. But he does not argue for his theory of list storage on the basis of aphasiological or other experimental evidence, or even discuss in general what kinds of evidence would support such a theory. On the other hand, it cannot be supposed that he was naive enough to believe that grammatical analysis alone and unaided could yield an accurate diagram of the brain's linguistic operations. This would be a quite implausible assumption, if only for the reason that the same word, phrase or sentence can easily be given different but equally defensible analyses by different grammarians.

The *Cours* shows Saussure to be uncomfortably aware of this problem, but he insists nevertheless – and quite firmly – that if grammar is to be a science it must be based on and reflect what is actually going on inside the speaker:

> One may say that the sum total of deliberate, systematic classifications set up by a grammarian studying a given linguistic state a-historically must coincide with the sum total of associations, conscious or unconscious, operative in speech. These are the associations which establish in the mind the various word families, flexional paradigms, formative elements (stems, suffixes, endings) etc.[17]

This is the first occasion in the history of Western theorising about language where one finds an unequivocal isomorphism postulated between the structure of some unobservable mechanism in the individual and the structure of some explicit systematisation established by a grammarian. And yet in the same breath – or more precisely, on the next page – the *Cours* laments that it is difficult to study these things, 'because one can never be sure whether the awareness of speakers of the language always goes as far as the grammarians' analyses'.

Now if indeed one can 'never be sure', then linguistics, by Saussure's own account, finds itself in quite a remarkable predicament. 'External' grammar is supposed to be descriptive of 'internal' grammar in the head, but at the same time it is

---

[17] ibid., p.189.

impossible to find out how accurate the description is. This is all the more remarkable in view of some of the grammatical analyses which Saussure himself proposes in the *Cours*. Nowhere does he suggest any test by which it might be possible to investigate whether his own analyses of French forms correspond to the distinctions 'consciously or unconsciously' adopted by the generality of native speakers of French.

In spite of this unresolved predicament, the general acceptance of Saussure's programme as providing the new 'modern' framework for linguistic inquiry laid an essential foundation for the later adoption of increasingly comprehensive mechanistic hypotheses about the workings of the unobservable 'internalised' system. Undoubtedly, one reason why the programme was congenial to many linguists of the day was the fact that it elected to begin linguistic inquiry at a carefully chosen starting-point where some of the most basic difficulties which beset any empirical investigation of human speech could conveniently be ignored. Saussure constantly assumes that speech can legitimately be treated as the oral counterpart of writing;[18] and, even more specifically, the counterpart of print. Saussurean linguistics is essentially the linguistics of 'typographic man', that curious subspecies of *homo sapiens* later identified by McLuhan.[19] Typographic man has not merely 'interiorised the alphabet' but interiorised it as a fount. Typographic man, in other words, is a communicator for whom the problem of types and tokens does not exist: just like Saussure's idealised *sujet parlant*.

It was Gutenberg's printing press, not Broca's laboratory, which provided Saussure with the models his linguistics needed. Mechanised printing with movable type differs from hand-writing in just those particulars which correspond to the differences between *langue* and *parole*. Although proclaiming the 'primacy of speech', Saussure's programme assumes that individual idiosyncrasies of pronunciation can safely be ignored. The Lockean theory of communication fails to provide any way of dealing with problems of the kind which might arise if speaker and hearer, through lack of mutual familiarity, found it hard to recognise each other's oral signals. There is no way, in other

[18] R.Harris, *The Language-Makers*, London 1980, p.16f.
[19] M.McLuhan, *The Gutenberg Galaxy*, Toronto 1962.

words, of coping with difficulties analogous to not being able to read someone else's handwriting. Printing is the answer. Saussurean linguistics proceeds from the outset as if speaker and hearer had available some oral analogue of the printed word. That none of Saussure's contemporaries seems to have found this odd as a basic assumption on which to found the study of spoken language reveals the full extent to which linguists of Saussure's generation were unconsciously committed to a text-based approach to language studies.

Although printing is often treated as just one among many forms of writing, from a communicational point of view it is more than that. In the communicational history of human culture, the advent of printing constitutes a revolution in its own right. For printing, in the sense which that term has acquired in European culture since Gutenberg, involves reliance on a unique technological achievement: the assurance of being able to reproduce by mechanical means 'the same' alphabetic forms. In part, that was due to Gutenberg's use of the screw press as a means of transferring ink to paper (as distinct from the manually held goose quill). But more important was the use of 'replica-casting from matrices which assured that in one and the same fount of type the same letters were not just similar but identical to each other, and that all letters could be set, evenly, on the level bed of the press so as to provide an absolutely flat printing surface.'[20]

Given the screw press and replica casting, Gutenberg launched printing on its historically unprecedented course. It was the spoken counterpart of typography that Saussure needed in order to construct a model of speech which measured up to the requirements pre-set by adopting a Lockean theory of speech communication. Printing meant being able to discount for all practical purposes the variation due to the individual scribe. That liberation had been achieved by purely mechanical means already in fifteenth-century Europe. But there was no corresponding liberation in oral communication, where the technology was simply lacking. It was lacking when Saussure was born, and still lacking when Saussure died. That is why there is no option but to regard Saussurean assumptions about oral standardisation as extrapolated from developments in a non-oral

[20] A.Gaur, *A History of Writing*, London 1984, p.203.

medium. Saussure, although ostensibly concerned with the theoretical foundations of his subject, never even raises the question of the legitimacy of this extrapolation.

Saussurean linguistics is also the linguistics of typographic man in a further and no less important respect. This relates to the actual production process, which differs fundamentally from that of writing because, as Ong puts it, 'the letters used in writing do not exist before the text in which they occur. With alphabetic letterpress print it is otherwise. Words are made out of units (types) which pre-exist as units before the words which they will constitute.'[21] This reduces the task of the post-Gutenberg typesetter to the simultaneous co-management of just two essential problems. There is no problem as regards devising a configuration which will unambiguously identify the letters of the alphabet. That problem has been pre-solved by replica-casting. The typesetter already has an ample reserve of ready-made replicas of every desired kind: all that is needed is a *selection* from this stock of replicas of the correct configuration. (The very terminology of what later became famous as Peirce's distinction between linguistic 'types' and 'tokens' serves as an eloquent reminder of its printing-press origins.) The typesetter's second problem is an extension of the first. At each available slot in the forme, another correct selection from the stock of replicas has to be made. What makes it a second problem is simply the interdependence of the selections: in other words, the overriding criterion is combinatorial. Correct selection for any particular slot depends on selections for the slots on either side.

This interlocking of 'horizontal' and 'vertical' selections is the conceptual prototype of Saussure's distinction between syntagmatic and associative relations. In this connexion, two 'typesetting' assumptions should be noted. One is that the typesetter's supply of replicas never runs out. The other is that a fount comprises a fixed number of characters. This is the limitation which in practice makes the typesetter's task manageable: it reduces to a search through a known inventory, of which the members are determined in advance. By working through this finite inventory, the typesetter must eventually find the character required to fill the next slot; and given an ample supply of replicas for every character, the slot can always be

---

[21] W.J.Ong, *Orality and Literacy*, New York 1982, p.118.

filled. In Saussurean linguistics there is no analogue to the problem of choosing between different founts: that would involve a third dimension of choice and a third set of linguistic relations, for which the simple Saussurean dichotomy 'syntagmatic vs. associative' makes no allowance. Nor is there any third dimension of choice available on the language frame at Lagado.

The only major difference between Saussure's account of linguistic structure and the machinery of the grand academy's language frame is that Saussure has taken another leaf out of Gutenberg's book by breaking down words into the oral equivalents of letters. Saussurean syntagmatics is thus double-decked: on the lower deck phonic elements are linearly combined into *signifiants*, while on the upper deck *signifiants* are linearly combined into syntagmas. The grand academy's project already starts on the 'upper deck' of syntagmatics, by taking the basically permutable elements to be the word forms of Balnibarbian, rather than the letters of the Balnibarbian alphabet. But perhaps Swift assumes that Balnibarbian writing is like Chinese rather than like English or Latin. If so, each character would correspond to something like a single *signifiant*, as opposed to a consonant or vowel. It does not affect the basic nature of the typesetting task. (In the East, Bi Sheng had already discovered the principle of movable type in the eleventh century, four hundred years before Gutenberg and without the benefit of an alphabet.) Whatever the fount, and whatever the 'direction' of lines of characters on the printed page, mechanised printing depends on two operations. One of these is the selection of a single character from a fixed inventory of characters, and the other is the linear concatenation of single characters thus selected. A text – defined in the printer's terms – is the product of a finite series of such selections, arranged in one continuous concatenation.

The Saussurean revolution in linguistics thus accomplished a number of interrelated things simultaneously. Perhaps most important of all it established the assumption (although not its legitimacy) that a 'scientific' linguistics must, for both practical and theoretical purposes, operate at a certain level of analysis and description. This level is in effect established by taking for granted that a number of what would otherwise be puzzling features of human language are somehow dealt with 'mechanically' in the human brain, and consequently do not constitute

problems for *linguistics* (however problematic they might be for
phoneticians, physiologists, psychologists and others, including
the lay language-user). Thus taken for granted are the
'mechanical' invariance of linguistic signs across manifest
differences in their acoustic signals and contexts of occurrence,
the 'mechanical' establishment of linguistic units, and the
'mechanical' establishment of combinatorial relations between
units, together with the invariant identification of both across
individuals and occasions. Unsurprisingly, it turns out that all
this conveniently hypothesised machinery in the brain yields a
hypothetically homogeneous linguistic community and a level of
discourse about its structures of communication which
corresponds almost exactly to the traditional European
metalanguage of grammar, but radically simplified in certain
respects. Saussure's real achievement as a theorist, although it
passed virtually unacknowledged by his contemporaries and
immediate successors, was to have shown how remarkably few
and simple were the basic postulates required to underpin this
level of discourse, with all its potential ramifications, and what
an unexpected explanatory weight it could be made to bear.[22]

* * *

It is worth insisting on the scriptist assumptions underlying
Saussurean linguistics for a number of reasons. One is that
Saussure himself constantly disavows them. For instance, he
goes to some lengths to point out how mistaken it is to confuse
spoken signs with their written representations. Having
described this common mistake as being 'rather as if people
believed that in order to find out what a person looks like it is
better to study his photograph than his face',[23] he evidently fails
to see that there is an even more serious mistake to be made:
namely, taking what the photograph shows as the correct basis
for an analysis of our visual perception of the face. This is the
mistake which is the analogue of his own adoption of a
typographical model in order to represent linguistic structure.
The consequence is that Saussure's concept of *parole* as
execution can hardly be better described than as an oral

[22] R.Harris, *Reading Saussure*, London 1987.
[23] Saussure, op.cit., p.45.

equivalent of the printing process, including the typesetting.

The extent to which this mistake also introduces conceptual confusion into the Saussurean account of *la langue* emerges when Saussure describes associative relations as relations *in absentia*, contrasting them with syntagmatic relations as relations *in praesentia*.[24] This misdescription is particularly revealing. It makes no sense at all unless tacitly referred to a written or printed model. For it is only on the visible page that the various elements of a syntagma appear to be all co-present: in speech their simultaneous occurrence is precluded by the Saussurean principle of linearity itself. Furthermore, what appear as co-present on the page are not elements of an activity, but the residual products of an activity: the marks or traces it leaves behind. Thus construing syntagmatic and associative relations in terms of the difference between 'presence' and 'absence' is doubly inappropriate for the analysis of speech. In the first place, it projects distinctions derived from one medium on to a quite different medium. In the second place, it projects distinctions derived from a product on to a process.

Having equipped his subject with this typographical model of linguistic structure, and a simple psychological mechanism of list storage to operate it, Saussure evidently thought there was nothing further to take into account as regards brain research. Forty years after Saussure's death, however, aphasiology was once again forcing itself upon the attention of linguists, general linguistics in the meanwhile having proceeded as if Broca had lived and died on another planet. This time it fell to Jakobson to defend the disciplinary independence (i.e. indifference) of the linguistic theorist, and the Jakobsonian defence is a classic example of academic history repeating itself. Jakobson argues[25] that in order to understand aphasia it is necessary to bring to bear the expert knowledge of many different specialists. The relevant fields of specialised expertise include, *mirabile dictu*, linguistics. And the special 'contribution' from linguistics turns out to be nothing other than Saussure's insistence that spoken language has a simple 'typographical' structure, which interlocks associative choices with syntagmatic choices. Thus history doth

[24] ibid., p.171.
[25] R.Jakobson, 'Two aspects of language and two types of aphasic disturbances'. In R.Jakobson and M.Halle, *Fundamentals of Language*, The Hague 1956.

make experts of us all. Saussure's refusal to come to terms with the aphasiology of his generation is resurrected a few decades later as his expert contribution to aphasiology.

As a linguist, Jakobson goes so far as to complain that aphasiologists have ignored 'the linguists' contribution to the investigation of aphasia'[26] – a quite remarkable accusation. According to Jakobson, 'the amazing progress of structural linguistics has endowed the investigator with efficient tools and methods for the study of verbal regression'.[27] How this 'amazing progress' could have benefited the ignorant aphasiologist is less than clear; but it will emerge, according to Jakobson, by 'the application of purely linguistic criteria to the interpretation and classification of aphasic facts' and submitting 'the clinical case reports to thorough linguistic analysis'.[28] (Exactly what a 'thorough linguistic analysis' meant by 1956 Jakobson does not specify.) Saussure might well have been surprised by Jakobson's recommendation that linguists, in addition to familiarising themselves with the medical disciplines dealing with aphasia, should themselves work with aphasic patients; but he would doubtless have been relieved to discover that this experience was not intended to improve the quality of their linguistic theorising.

The way Jakobson sets about applying 'purely linguistic criteria' to aphasia is, to say the least, highly restrictive. On the one hand, Jakobson claims for linguistics a concern with language 'in all its aspects – language in operation, language in drift, language in its nascent state, and language in dissolution'.[29] On the other hand, – and this is the basis of the complaint that aphasiologists have ignored linguistics – it appears that this concern is limited to such matters as can be usefully analysed in terms of the single contrast between syntagmatic and associative relations. It is rather like claiming that acupuncture is concerned with all conditions of the body, in sickness or in health, but that it does not deal with those conditions except insofar as they may be analysable in terms of the opposition between yin and yang. There is a retreat, in other words, from the programmatic assertion that linguistics is 'the' science of language to the apparently more modest – but at the

---

[26] ibid., p.55.
[27] ibid., p.56.
[28] ibid., p.56.
[29] ibid., p.55.

same time more arrogant – assumption that linguistics deals with language in the only scientifically valid way. (Otherwise, why would this particular way of dealing with language phenomena be entitled to the designation *linguistics*?)

Unsurprisingly, Jakobson proceeds to distinguish just two basic types of aphasia, which he calls 'similarity disorder' and 'contiguity disorder'. In the former type it is the patient's 'selective capacity' which is impaired, while in the latter it is the 'gift for combination'. 'Combination' and 'selection' are Jakobson's preferred terms for the 'two modes of arrangement' characteristic of the linguistic sign, which give rise to the relationships of 'contiguity' and 'similarity' respectively:

> The addressee perceives that the given utterance (message) is a *combination* of constituent parts *selected* from the repository of all possible constituent parts (code). The constituents of a context are in a status of *contiguity*, while in a substitution set signs are linked by various degrees of *similarity*...[30]

Here we have the Saussurean schema of linguistic structure garbed a generation later in new terminology. Unfortunately, what the new terminology blurs is Saussure's crucial distinction between *langue* and *parole*: for the term *combination* subsumes both combinations which depend on the choice of the individual speaker and those which do not, and likewise, *mutatis mutandis*, for its terminological partner *selection*. The result is that Jakobson's model, although based on Saussure, ends up by obscuring the very contribution which Saussurean linguistics might have offered aphasiology (by distinguishing disorders of *langue* from disorders of *parole*).

Even less surprising in consequence is Jakobson's discovery that it is unproblematic to classify any case of aphasia as involving 'similarity disorder', 'contiguity disorder' or a combination of the two. On this basis, he concludes that although the specific 'varieties of aphasia are numerous and diverse', nevertheless 'all of them oscillate between the two polar types'.[31] But given that the proposed analysis allows only two kinds of linguistic relationship in the first place, it is difficult to see what other classification of 'disorders' would be available.

[30] ibid., p.61.
[31] ibid., p.76.

2. The Gutenberg Connexion

What is solemnly presented as an empirical contribution to aphasiology turns out to be merely a simplistic categorisation derived from Saussure's model of the language machine.

Confusion is even worse confounded when Jakobson takes over Saussure's misinterpretation of associative relations as relations *in absentia*, and of syntagmatic relations as relations *in praesentia*.[32] This assimilation is singularly inappropriate for the analysis of aphasia, in view of the fact that the one essential requirement for the *presence* of any given syntagmatic unit in non-aphasic speech is precisely the *absence* of any other syntagmatic unit. That is to say, the basic task of the speaker in normal speech is to organise the correctly sequenced non-simultaneous and non-overlapping presentation of the syntagmatic units. Simultaneous co-presentation is a feature of words on the page, not of words in speech. Syntagmatically normal articulation necessarily involves the management of a continuous flow of temporal transitions, for which the static sentence on the page cannot but provide an inadequate and misleading model. The difference is as fundamental as the difference between a tableau and a play. A scene acted out on the stage is not a rapid succession of tableaux. It comprises *events*. That is why no model of drama based on the tableau is in principle adequate as a basis for analysing the kind of stagecraft required to perform a play. It is for similar reasons difficult to understand the justification for adopting a model for speech analysis which incorporates precisely this error. Such a model denies in advance the possibility that disorders of transitional flow will be found to constitute an independent aphasiological category, and already dictates their subsumption under 'contiguity disorders'.

More significant than these details, however, is the general assumption underlying Jakobson's paper. It is that although aphasiologists have as one of their continuing professional concerns a progressively more detailed documentation of the malfunctions of the human 'language machine', the definitive account of the 'language machine' in working order is already available and needed only armchair reflection on the matter by linguistic theorists. The idea that linguists might better understand the workings of their theoretically postulated

---

[32] ibid., p.61.

machine by considering the evidence of its malfunctioning in cases of aphasia is not even raised (any more than the question of whether it is legitimate to transpose *a priori* distinctions of linguistic theory into the empirical study of speech disorders). Gutenberg doubtless never imagined that his screw press would exert such intellectual pressure.

Chapter Three
The Syntax Machine

The Professor of Glottomechanics at Lagado would have found Saussure's *Cours* an unhelpful manual in one respect. Although it supplies confirmation that the Balnibarbian language frame is constructed in principle along the right lines with its two mechanised dimensions of linguistic choice, the *Cours* gives few hints about how to tackle syntax as an engineering problem. The *mécanisme de la langue* provides for the automatic production of word forms like *marchons*, but does not provide for the automatic production of sentences as such. Yet one can hardly suppose Saussure thought that the speaker, or the speaker's brain, assembles a sentence by the crude technique of trial and error. Doubtless we do often in speaking or writing experience difficulty in 'finding the right words'; but if our difficulties were of the order attendant upon the random turning of forty cerebral handles we might well spend days trying to come up with a coherent phrase, for exactly the same reason as it might have taken the professor's assistants whom Gulliver saw at work in Lagado just as long to find one. The *Cours* says very little about this problem. The list storage principle of Saussure's associative dimension in itself offers no guarantee that linguistic units are filed for easy accessibility; nor does the bare linearity of Saussurean syntagmatics suggest a method for tackling the combinatorial task. In fact, Saussure does not distinguish at all clearly between questions pertaining to the content and organisation of the associative-cum-syntagmatic system (*la langue*) and questions pertaining to the processes which presumably make use of the system in the articulation and analysis of discourse (*la parole*). Saussure's skeletal outline of the *mécanisme* in our brains leaves a great deal of detail to be filled in.

By the 1950s linguistic theorists had come round to a way of

61

thinking which was far more sympathetic to the Professor of Glottomechanics' problem. In part this was due to the influence of cybernetics and information theory. In his 1956 paper, Jakobson wrote approvingly:

> The communication engineer most properly approaches the essence of the speech event when he assumes that in the optimal exchange of information the speaker and the listener have at their disposal more or less the same 'filing cabinet of *prefabricated* representations': the addresser of a verbal message selects one of these 'preconceived possibilities' and the addressee is supposed to make an identical choice from the same assembly of 'possibilities already foreseen and provided for'.[1]

But the ground had already been prepared in advance for this acceptance of the communication engineer's approach by a significant development in linguistic theory: the advent of distributionalism.[2] The distributionalist approach to language has been aptly if unflatteringly described as 'the development of certain aspects of Bloomfieldianism to their extremes'.[3] Specifically, it extends a 'building-block style of description … into the higher levels of grammar'.[4] Alternatively, one might say that it reduces the architecture of the sentence to simple brick-laying.

What is wrong with the machine Gulliver inspected is that it fails to come to terms with a simple fact about Balnibarbian which can be summed up in four words: 'Not all combinations occur'. This epigrammatic formulation was originally offered not as an observation on the grand academy's mechanisation project, but as a statement of linguistic theory by the founder of distributionalism, Zellig Harris. The basic principles of syntagmatic structure, in other words, are principles of combinatorial restriction. Were it otherwise linguistic description would be a trivially simple matter:

> If all combinations of our elements occurred, there would be nothing to say except a listing of the elements and the statement

---

[1] ibid., p.58.

[2] R.Harris, *The Language-Makers*, London 1980, p.163ff.

[3] R.H.Robins, *A Short History of Linguistics*, 2nd ed., London 1979, p.210.

[4] M.Joos, *Readings in Linguistics I. The Development of Descriptive Linguistics in America 1925-1956*, 4th ed., Chicago 1966, p.115.

that all combinations of them occur...[5]

By the same token, the language frame at Lagado would need no improvement: it would already work. Every turn of the forty handles would produce impeccable Balnibarbian sentences.

For the distributionalist, then, grammar reduces to a set of restrictions on the co-occurrence of linguistic items sequentially concatenated. This means that the basic model of syntax is exactly that adopted by the academicians of Lagado. Their language frame in effect represents the sentence as a simple linear string of elements. The structure of the string has its physical embodiment in the wire along which the pieces of wood bearing the words of Balnibarbian are strung. *String* was later to become a technical term in linguistic theory: it is defined in a recent dictionary of linguistic terminology as

> a term used in linguistics, and especially in generative grammar, to refer to a linear sequence of elements of determinate length and constitution.[6]

That description fits exactly what appears along any single wire of the contrivance which Gulliver admired. The same dictionary goes on to define the term *substring* as

> any part of a string which is itself a string. For example, the following sentence can be seen as a string of elements: *the + cat + sit + Past + on + the + mat*. Within this, several substrings could be recognized, e.g. *the + cat, the + cat + sit + Past*, etc.

Thus what the professor's assistants at Lagado spent six hours a day doing could be quite precisely described in modern linguistic terminology as trying to generate by mechanical means substrings which could be read as parts of Balnibarbian sentences.

The only difference between the strings on the frame and the strings recognised by modern linguistic theorists is that the latter contain elements like *Past*. That is to say, the string and substring cited in the above example presuppose that *the cat sat* has already been analysed into the four elements *the + cat + sit*

[5] Z.S.Harris, *Methods in Structural Linguistics*, Chicago 1951, p.150.
[6] D.Crystal, *A Dictionary of Linguistics and Phonetics*, 2nd ed., Oxford 1985, p.290.

+ *Past*, which involves a somewhat curious convention (of which more below) that treats the past tense form of the English verb *sit* as a linear combination of two units. At Lagado, by contrast, the academy's machine operated with the elements unanalysed in this way. As Swift tells us in the passage cited above, the Balnibarbian words were represented 'in their several moods, tenses and declensions', which seems to indicate that a similar machine for English would have shown *sat* as a simple indivisible form, rather than as the two separate elements *sit* and *Past*.

Ignoring for the moment details of this kind, it is obvious that once the problem is conceptualised mechanically along these lines it will fall necessarily into two parts. First, operations will be needed to locate the required linguistic units (*cat, mat, on*, etc.) and, second, operations will be needed to assemble those units into appropriate combinations. Intuitively, it seems indeed that these must be two quite different problems. The difficulty of 'thinking of' the words *cat, mat*, etc. when we need them seems to be psychologically a quite different difficulty from that of avoiding saying *The mat sat on the cat*, or *The sat mat on the cat*, or *The on the cat sat mat* or any of many other jumbles which a random assembly process might produce. That linguistic theorists do indeed regard getting strings of elements in the right order as a problem for speakers is evident from a title such as that of one paper presented in 1981 at a Royal Society and British Academy symposium on 'The Psychological Mechanisms of Language'. The paper in question was called 'The speaker's linearization problem',[7] and it subdivides this problem in turn into two. There is a purely conceptual part belonging to the realm of *ratio* and a purely linguistic part belonging to the realm of *oratio*. This distinction explicitly follows that already drawn by Ramus in the sixteenth century. From Swift's description it is evident that the academicians of Lagado regarded the second (*oratio*) as the more urgent practical problem. If only the machine could generate sentences, the task of putting those sentences into some kind of rational order would at least be approachable. Even if, on the other hand, we treat the problem of linearisation in *ratio* as primary, there still appears to remain a problem in the organisation of *oratio*, which is the analogue of the forty handles.

---

[7] W.J.M.Levelt, 'The speaker's linearization problem', *The Psychological Mechanisms of Language*, London 1981.

We may note at this point that to equate syntax with the assembly of given units is nowadays to invite a description of the process in terms of machinery. Saussurean linearity is easily imagined as a conveyor belt on which completed verbal items must eventually issue forth from the assembly process properly fitted together. To describe how that happens is to describe the assembly process itself. But it is also important to note that once we adopt this way of looking at the matter the notion of 'assembly process' acquires a certain ambiguity, and this ambiguity answers exactly to a problem in Saussurean syntagmatics. Are we dealing with a design process or a production process?

The difference is important, for it corresponds to two ways of thinking about sentential 'constructions' like *The cat sat on the mat*. The design of this sentence is a certain interrelationship of the units *cat, mat, on*, etc., and a description of the design process will reveal the principles according to which these units are put together in order to function as parts of the sentence. The production of the sentence, on the other hand, is a matter of achieving the desired design in the form of a completed object, given the initial set of unordered units.

Design problems and production problems cannot be completely divorced in any mechanical enterprise. For it would obviously be foolish to design an artifact based on unit construction without taking into consideration at all whether or not the design would give rise to severe or even insuperable production problems. Nevertheless, design problems are of a different order from production problems, even though dispute may legitimately arise over which are which in particular cases. (In modern industrial jargon, production problems are often taken to include difficulty in obtaining the parts; but this is really an external supply problem which has nothing to do with the factory production process as such.)

As regards language, the distinction between design and production is reflected to a certain extent, but not sys-tematically, in the terminology of traditional grammar. Terms like *subject* and *object* are design terms. Terms like *prefix* and *suffix* are production terms. When Aristotle gave his celebrated definitions of *onoma* and *rhema*, and then added the observation that it was possible to transpose the two units in combination without thereby altering the meaning,[8] he was already acknowledging the distinction between a design process and a production process. Indeed, he was in effect identifying *onoma* and *rhema* as what later theorists of mechanics were to call a 'kinetic pair'.

The Greeks from a very early period evidently conceived of language in terms of assembly processes, as the term *syntax* itself indicates. Furthermore, since the Greek term for a linguistic element (*stoicheíon*) was also a term applied to primary elements of the physical universe,[9] the question is not whether they saw any parallel between the interconnexion of linguistic elements and the interconnexion of physical elements, but rather how far this parallel extended. (For the Greeks, the machine had not yet become a general model of the physical universe. This was essentially a post-Renaissance development. As Boirel points out, the Aristotelian dichotomy between 'natural' and 'violent' motion stands in the way of treating the world *in toto* as a machine, and it was not until Tartaglia's work on ballistics in the sixteenth century that the Aristotelian doctrine was seriously compromised.[10])

By the time the concept of the human language machine had reached its Saussurean phase of elaboration, any distinction between design processes and production processes in language had become very hazy. It was a distinction for which nineteenth-century comparative and historical linguistics had had no use at all because the dominant metaphor throughout that period in linguistics had been not mechanical but organic. In the case of Saussure himself, it is not altogether clear whether he failed to see the distinction between design and production as being important or whether he thought that for linguistic theory other distinctions were even more important. Certainly he insisted on two ideas which have a direct bearing on details of both design and production, although his presentation of these two ideas may have obscured the connexion. One of them was his own theoretical dichotomy between *langue* and *parole*, and the other was the notion of the linearity of the linguistic sign. It would be out of place to examine either of these Saussurean *topoi* in detail here,[11]

[8] *De Interpretatione*, 20b.
[9] F.E.Peters, *Greek Philosophical Terms*, New York 1967, p.180ff.
[10] R.Boirel, *Le mécanisme hier et aujourd'hui*, Paris 1982, pp.14-15.
[11] Cf. R.Harris, *Reading Saussure*, London 1987.

but the following points are pertinent to the present discussion.

Saussure appears to have held that an individual who utters a sentence has no control over its design, but has certain responsibilities related to its production. It would be a mistake on that account, however, to identify production processes with neurophysiological events in particular brains. ('How can a community produce a sentence?' it may be asked. 'Only a language-user can do that. Therefore production processes belong to *parole*.' But to see why this will not do, we have only to recall Aristotle's observation about the transposition of *onoma* and *rhema*.) What Saussure does not tell us is exactly which features of production are involved in the act of *parole*. He refuses to recognise the sentence itself as a unit of *langue*, and claims that in syntagmatics no clear boundary between *langue* and *parole* can be drawn. For a later generation, Saussure's dichotomy has been further obfuscated by superimposing upon it not only the generativist distinction between linguistic 'competence' and linguistic 'performance' (itself a muddle[12]), but also the Peircean distinction between linguistic 'types' and linguistic 'tokens'. In this connexion perhaps the most important point to grasp is that even if Saussure had recognised the validity of treating *The cat sat on the mat* as a sentence-type, that would in no way have committed him to recognising it *eo ipso* as a unit of *langue*.[13] Furthermore, although one might ask relevant production questions about a Peircean token, it is far from clear that it makes any sense at all to ask design questions about a Peircean type.

As regards linearity, what gives rise to misunderstanding is Saussure's unfortunate penchant for explaining it by appealing to what sound very like constraints of a purely physical or physiological nature. The *Cours* speaks of the impossibility of pronouncing two things at once, and this can easily be taken to be a rather trite observation to the effect that the articulatory organs cannot be in more than one position at a time. True though that is, it is irrelevant: a painter's brush cannot be in more than one position at a time either, but that does not entail that the structure of a painting must be linear. Likewise, Saussure's references to linearity as a 'temporal' feature of

[12] R.Harris, *The Language Myth*, London 1981, p.34.
[13] C.M.Hutton, *The type-token relation: abstraction and instantiation in linguistic theory*, Oxford 1986.

speech suggest that linearity is merely a matter of chronological succession. Again, true though it is that *The cat sat on the mat* is a sentence which takes a finite length of time to utter, that fact itself does not impose linearity of structure any more than the fact that it takes the painter a finite length of time to execute brush strokes on the canvas imposes a linearity of structure upon the painting. If considerations of this order were the determinants of linearity, Saussure's principle of linguistic structure would collapse into the general truism that all human activities take place in a spatio-temporal continuum and the human body, as a spatio-temporally extended object, cannot be in several different positions or places simultaneously. In that sense, everything we do, including speaking, would have to be 'linear'.

Saussure's principle of the linearity of the linguistic sign is not a banality of this order, even though readers of the *Cours* may be encouraged to think so by Saussure's casual claim that its truth is perfectly obvious (which has not prevented some of Saussure's critics from disputing it). Saussurean linearity is the linearity Aristotle invokes in his observation about the transposition of *onoma* and *rhema*. That is to say, it is a joint condition of both production and design, identifying the basic level at which production requirements and design requirements coincide. And that is far from a banality, since there is nothing about the spatio-temporal continuum in which we live which requires a communication system to meet this condition. That language does conform to the condition seems perfectly obvious once it is pointed out. But, as Saussure goes on to observe, no one has yet systematically worked out all its linguistic consequences. (This he evidently regards as a future task for general linguistics.[14]) In the meantime, Saussure accepts linearity as a 'mechanical' principle of language assembly, and accordingly makes the syntagma an integral part of his *mécanisme de la langue*.

These preliminary considerations are relevant to an appreciation of the fact that fully 'automated' sentence production is – and is intended to be – quite beyond the capacity of the postulated Saussurean language machine in the brain. Speaking, for Saussure, is not a matter of merely giving vocal utterance to

---

[14] The only linguistic theorist to pursue it with any rigour after Saussure was Guillaume, to whom linguistics owes the term *psychomécanique*.

mental sentences which come already assembled. A far more powerful language machine would be needed for that. Distributionalism holds out the prospect of such a machine, operating on principles which are simpler than Saussure's, and requiring virtually no 'thought' on the part of the user. Distributionalism still recognises two dimensions of linguistic 'choice', but Saussure's complex array of associative relations and syntagmatic relations is replaced by a simple grid of substitution relations and co-occurrence relations. The possibilities of 'choice' available are totally determined by this grid. The great difference with Saussure's interlocking mechanism for associations and syntagmas is that both associative and syntagmatic relations, for Saussure, involve meaning; whereas distributional analysis dispenses with meaning altogether, treating linguistic structure as purely syntactic in nature. This elimination of meaning (a policy in line with then fashionable behaviourist theories in psychology, and officially espoused by Bloomfield in the 1930s as the only 'scientific' basis for linguistics) left linguists with nothing synchronic to describe *except* sequential patterns of substitution and co-occurrence. Thus whereas Saussurean linguistics deals with structural properties which *may* be described (partly) in terms of mechanical operations, distributional linguistics deals with structural properties which cannot be described *other than* in terms of mechanical operations. The language machine had thus by the 1950s acquired a new status in linguistics: it had made itself – for American distributionalists at least – descriptively indispensable.

At the same time the distributionalists refused to speculate about the possible 'psychological reality' of the sentence structures they described. To have sought or proclaimed any Saussurean 'correspondence' between the grammarian's external analyses and the speaker's internal analyses would have flouted the basic tenets of behaviourism. A machine, as far as the distributionalists were concerned, was simply one possible model for the descriptive 'presentation' of linguistic structure.[15] Its role as a model for their own analytic procedures the distributionalists passed over in silence.

Granted an unquestioning acceptance of distributionalist

---

[15] Z.S.Harris, op. cit., p.373.

assumptions, it is clear that syntax does become a relatively simple engineering problem. The distributionalist programme for the Professor of Glottomechanics at Lagado will incorporate the following recommendations. 1. Sort the forms of Balnibarbian into substitution classes.[16] 2. Adjust the wires on the frame to take sentences of various lengths (one-word, two-word, three-word, etc.). 3. Subcategorise the substitution classes for sentences of different lengths. 4. Ensure that the forms appearing on the various surfaces of any one revolving piece of wood are either identical or else members of the same substitutional subcategory. A frame organised according to these principles can at least guarantee that every turn of the forty handles produces forty Balnibarbian sentences. A comparable machine for English might produce, for example, the following alternatives along a given wire: *The cat sat on the mat, The dog sat on the mat, A cat sat on the carpet, The dog stood on a rug, The rabbit stood on the carpet*, and many more, simply by ensuring the relevant permutations of (i) *a* and *the*, (ii) *cat, dog* and *rabbit*, (iii) *sat* and *stood*, and (iv) *rug, mat* and *carpet*. Such a programme would ideally require the Professor of Glottomechanics to construct many frames of different sizes with different vocabularies; but an escalation of the research project was already recognised as urgent at the time of Gulliver's visit.

It cannot be denied that if the Professor of Glottomechanics built a distributionalist multi-frame syntax machine it would mark a genuine advance in his mechanisation programme. The previously wasted labour of trial and error would be eliminated at one stroke. What may be less obvious is that the reason why the machine can achieve this advance is that it can treat all syntactic assembly processes as production processes. In other words, it can afford to ignore meaning because the selection of sentences for their meaning belongs to the later stage of constructing Balnibarbian books of 'philosophy, poetry, politicks, law, mathematicks and theology'. This explains how, for example, the machine can assemble a sentence such as *The cat sat on the mat* without the benefit of any analyses of the kind given by traditional grammars or dictionaries; for what matters 'mechanically' is not the function of any given word in a sentence

---

[16] By applying the procedures explained in Ch.15 of *Methods in Structural Linguistics*, so that all the forms of each class 'substitute for each other in approximately every environment of that class' (op. cit., p.251).

(i.e. the sentence design), but simply whether or not it can occur next to another given word or words in a given sequential position. There are never more than two values ('+' and '−'; 'yes' or 'no') to be taken into account for any syntagmatic position: given any word in the vocabulary of Balnibarbian, either it can occur in this position (value '+') or it cannot occur in this position (value '−'). The distributional definition of a word is thus the sum total of its possibilities of occurrence ('+' or '−') in sequence with other words. In effect, such a definition will be a set of rules saying where the word may and may not occur. By the same token, each distributional 'rule of grammar' will say which sets of words (or other linguistic units) may co-occur sequentially or be substituted in given sequential positions. Grammar is thus reduced to sequential production. Better still, modern 'information theory'[17] shows how it is possible, given any set of sentences, to calculate the mathematical probabilities of transition from one word to another in the sequence. All of which suits the Professor of Glottomechanics down to the ground. That is just the type of linguistic theory his project needs.

* * *

More versatile machines, but based on the same principles, will become available for the Professor of Glottomechanics if he is prepared to abandon old-fashioned frames and wires altogether; for frames and wires physically restrict the types of operation that can be performed on sentential 'strings'. He might consider approaching the project of mechanisation from the opposite end by asking: 'What kind of machine do I need to build in order to handle the permutations which will be most useful in producing all the varieties of Balnibarbian sentence?' This is exactly the type of question which came to be raised in distributional theory in the mid-1950s. It is a question, patently, which still conceptualises the problem of syntax as a mechanical problem of *oratio*. We find it formulated explicitly in the following terms:

[17] For sophistications of this order, the Professor of Glottomechanics would have had to wait until the publication of C.L.Shannon and W.Weaver, *The Mathematical Theory of Communication*, Urbana, 1949, although Swift tells us that the mathematics of mechanisation had not escaped the attention of the grand academy. The designer of the language frame Gulliver inspected had already made 'the strictest computation of the general proportion' between the various parts of speech found in texts.

> Assuming the set of grammatical English sentences to be given,
> we now ask what sort of device can produce this set (equivalently,
> what sort of theory gives an adequate account of the structure of
> this set of utterances).[18]

This formulation is interesting not only for its overtly 'engineering' approach to grammar but also for the equation it specifically makes between a device and a theory. These correspond respectively to 'machine' and 'blueprint'. A theory is envisaged as a kind of pen-on-paper equivalent of a device. Correspondingly, the device or machine is envisaged as a theory manifested in material form. The equation is worthy of note, for in 'real' engineering it is an equation which would never be made. A blueprint is not a machine, and a theory of blueprints is something quite different from a theory of machines. Once that difference is ignored, however, it will become legitimate to discuss the blueprints *as if they were* the machines; and, *pari passu*, discuss grammars as if they were mental realities. As an assumption underlying *linguistic* theorising, this is particularly problematic, since it already begs certain basic questions about language and the metalinguistic representation of language.

More important, however, is the fact that the formulation of the question marks a new, third stage of evolution in the myth of the language machine. It is a stage never before reached by any of the earlier metaphors used by linguists or philosophers in the Western tradition of linguistic inquiry. All other linguistic metaphors (the contract metaphor, the organism metaphor, the tool metaphor, the institutional metaphor, etc.) remain conceptually independent of – and hence clearly recognisable *as metaphorical* with respect to – the detailed descriptive representation of linguistic phenomena. They are global or external metaphors, which apply only in general and at a certain rather vague level of abstraction. No one asks, for instance, 'Which clause of the linguistic contract governs nouns and verbs?' or 'Which cells of the linguistic organism synthesise sentences?' And if such questions were to be asked they could not be taken seriously, because there is neither a metaphorical nor a metalinguistic basis for taking them seriously. With the machine metaphor the case is quite different, and for reasons

[18] A.N.Chomsky, *Syntactic Structures*, The Hague 1957, p.18.

which relate directly to the post-Renaissance development of technology in Western culture. In 1457 it might well have sounded absurd to ask 'What sort of machine can produce this set of sentences?' But by 1957 it did not. Modern thinking about language and the mind was already mesmerised by its own mythology.

As far as our Professor of Glottomechanics is concerned, none of this need occasion the least doubt or query. Once the general question of grammatical structure is posed in terms of possible machines, he cannot fail to take the keenest interest in how it will eventually be answered. The following proposal envisages a machine which is both similar to but also in certain respects different from the original frame at Lagado.

> Suppose we have a machine that can be in any one of a finite number of different internal states, and suppose that this machine switches from one state to another by producing a certain symbol (let us say, an English word). One of these states is an initial state; another is a final state. Suppose that the machine begins in the initial state, runs through a sequence of states (producing a word with each transition), and ends in the final state. Then we call the sequence of words that has been produced a 'sentence'. Each such machine thus defines a certain language; namely the set of sentences that can be produced in this way.[19]

The trouble with the original language machine at Lagado, put in these terms, was that the set of sentences it produced did not match the sentences of Balnibarbian, even though the machine was programmed with the entire Balnibarbian vocabulary. In short, the language defined by the grand academy's apparatus was simply not Balnibarbian, even though the units it operated with were words of the Balnibarbian language.

Not until the syntax of sentences is thought of as determined by the operations of a machine does it become a much acclaimed 'breakthrough' in linguistic theory to observe that a simple generating device of the particular type described above[20] (generating one word at a time and putting it next to the word previously generated) will not deal very satisfactorily with certain syntactic processes encountered in English (and doubtless in Balnibarbian too). And only then can the

[19] Chomsky, op. cit., pp.18-19.
[20] Known to mathematicians as a 'finite state Markov process'.

specification of a more powerful type of machine, capable of handling more complex processes, come to be hailed as the foundation of an entirely new kind of grammatical analysis. The 'transformational-generative' linguistics developed in the late 1950s – appropriately enough at the Massachusetts Institute of Technology – was a distributional linguistics reformulated specifically in terms of the capacity of machines.

Along with this mechanical conceptualisation of syntax goes a new definition of 'a language':

> a set (finite or infinite) of sentences, each finite in length, and constructed out of a finite set of elements.[21]

In this sense, clearly, even the haphazard word-sequences produced by the language machine of Lagado belong to a language: it simply happens to be the wrong language for the grand academy's purposes. Correspondingly, a 'grammar' of 'a language' becomes not, as is usually understood, a set of precepts formulated by a grammarian, but simply, for any language L:

> a device that generates all of the grammatical sequences of L and none of the ungrammatical ones.[22]

That is to say, the syntax generator *is* the grammar. And once we have the notion that sentences are the products of 'language-generating automata', it is but a short step to the notion that the set of rules *constitutes* the automaton.[23]

This radical reinterpretation of traditional terms is another diagnostic by which we may recognise that the myth of the language machine has now reached a new, critical phase unprecedented in the conceptual history of any other linguistic metaphor. Of far greater significance, however, are the consequences of this terminological reinterpretation. They lead directly to a complete conceptual divorce between language and linguistic communities. A language is no longer envisaged as needing human language-users at all, or a human brain to house it, as long as it has a machine to generate it; and its sentences need serve no social or communicational purpose of any kind. Or,

[21] Chomsky, op. cit., p.13.
[22] Chomsky, loc. cit.
[23] Chomsky, op. cit., p.20.

equivalently, language continues to be treated as a function of language-users, but the language-users are deprived of their status as human beings: it becomes legitimate for purposes of linguistic theory to 'view the speaker as being essentially a machine'.[24] What is remarkable about this development is how the linguistic and the mechanical, now treated as interdependent, thereby achieve a symbiosis which is entirely autonomous. The syntax machine of 1957 has no other function than to generate 'sentences', and the 'sentences' have no other status than that of 'products' of an otherwise purposeless machine. The effect of the symbiosis is a total decontextualisation of language, unique in the Western tradition.

Even more remarkable was the warm welcome this received from those philosophers who hastened to congratulate linguists on having dispensed altogether with the assumption 'that the corpus of utterances studied by the linguist was produced by a conscious organism'.[25] The reason why they were so pleased is clear. They saw this great 'advance' in linguistics at last letting them off the painful hook of the 'mind-body' problem altogether.

---

[24] M.Gross and A.Lentin, *Introduction to Formal Grammars*, London 1970, p.111.
[25] H.Putnam, 'Minds and machines' p.95. In *Dimensions of Mind: A Symposium*, ed. S.Hook, New York 1960. Reprinted in A.R.Anderson (ed.), *Minds and Machines*, Englewood Cliffs 1964. (Page reference to the reprint.)

Chapter Four
The Mechanisation of Meaning

The fourth and final phase in the myth of the language machine is the mechanisation of meaning.

It need hardly be stressed that any syntactic generator of the 1957 vintage described above will perform abysmally in the Turing test. Even if equipped to produce a syntactically correct English sentence in response to each of the questions put by Turing's investigator, the machine has no means of distinguishing which of its sentences would be appropriate or inappropriate. More basically still, the machine does not distinguish between sense and nonsense. It is as likely to produce Lewis Carroll sentences like *The walrus sat on the radiator* as it is to produce unproblematic albeit less exciting sentences like *The cat sat on the mat*. But then it is just as likely to produce *The cat sat on the mat* as a 'reply' to 'What is the length of your hair?' as to 'When was the battle of Hastings?'.

At this level the project of the Professor of Glottomechanics again links up with Turing's imitation game. Writing a book in Balnibarbian makes no linguistic demands which are essentially different from taking a Balnibarbian Turing test. Both will require a command of the vocabulary and grammar of the language. Both will require a fund of information about how to use the language to express a great variety of ideas in coherent and relevant sequence. Any book may be regarded, if we wish, as the author's edited record of replies to an imaginary, self-imposed Turing test, but with the questions omitted. For example, the following sequence of four hypothetical Turing-test questions

Where do we start?
What was there?
Where was it?
Can you be more precise?

yield, as an edited transcript of one possible set of replies, the first verse of the gospel according to St John:

> In the beginning was the Word, and the Word was with God, and the Word was God.

Dispensing with the question-and-answer format, or supplying it hypothetically, does not in the end affect our judgment as to whether or not the first verse of John's gospel is likely to have been produced by an intelligent being. To ignore this is to fail to see that the underlying rationale of the Turing test has nothing to do specifically with its quiz programme presentation. Asking and answering questions is only one kind of language game.

It was a different language game which was to become one of the principal focuses of interest after the second world war. This was the language game of translation. During the late 1940s and 1950s, for both military and commercial reasons, it came to be regarded as increasingly desirable to see whether machines could play this game, thus eliminating or reducing reliance on human translators. In part, the impetus to tackle the problem was carried over from the concentrated effort on techniques of cryptography developed during the war. In this context it seemed quite natural to regard a language as simply another (rather haphazardly organised) coding system, and relationships between languages as analogous to relationships between codes. A text in a foreign language could be regarded, Warren Weaver once remarked, as 'really written in English, but... coded in some strange symbols'.[1] Although it rapidly came to be realised that this was not in practice a useful hypothesis, the enterprise of machine translation never entirely left behind this initial 'cryptographic psychology'.

The more perceptive researchers saw, however, that their projects were concerned 'not so much with a new machine as with a new analysis of linguistic phenomena'.[2] The entire automatic translation programme of this period provides a striking example of the ways in which a combination of changing socio-political pressures and technological progress can force traditional linguistic assumptions to be questioned or simply abandoned. Given the background of the Cold War, it is no

[1] E.Delavenay, *An Introduction to Machine Translation*, London 1960, p.8.
[2] Delavenay, op. cit., p.1.

surprise that 'translation from Russian into English has high priority',[3] or that the introductory chapter to one of the classic surveys of machine translation had the title 'Translation in the Atomic Age'. Its author remarks:

> The problem of translation, which has faced modern man ever since the Renaissance has, like many other problems, taken on new aspects in the light of the geographical shifts of power apparent at the outset of the atomic era.[4]

This was also evidently the view of funding agencies both in the USA and, somewhat later, in the USSR. In the latter case, this also entailed a dramatic revision in the socio-political assessment of linguistics. According to Bar-Hillel, structural linguistics in Soviet Russia had hitherto

> unfailingly been condemned as idealistic, bourgeois and formalistic. However, when the Russion government awakened from its dogmatic slumber to the tune of the Georgetown University demonstration of machine translation in January 1954, structural linguistics became within a few weeks a discipline of high prestige and priority.[5]

In the USA by 1951, to judge by Bar-Hillel's survey of machine translation published in that year,[6] it was generally assumed that machines would be needed which were capable of at least the following linguistic tasks: (i) the mechanical analysis of each word in the source language, giving the stem of the word and its morphological category, (ii) the mechanical identification of syntactic units within a given sentence, on the basis of the morphological categories of the constituent words and their order, and (iii) the mechanical transformation of a given sentence 'into another that is logically equivalent to it',[7] and rearrangement of the transform to match the normal word-order

[3] Delavenay, op. cit., p.31.

[4] Delavenay, op. cit., p.2.

[5] Y.Bar-Hillel, 'Four lectures on algebraic linguistics and machine translation', 1962. Reprinted in Y.Bar-Hillel, *Language and Information*, Reading, Mass. 1964. Page references to this and other papers by Bar-Hillel are to *Language and Information*.

[6] Y.Bar-Hillel, 'The state of machine translation in 1951'. Reprinted in Bar-Hillel, op.cit., pp.153-65.

[7] Bar-Hillel, op. cit., p.158.

of the target language. It is this third requirement which moves the enterprise beyond the possibility of solutions which, given highly 'regular' languages with well marked morphological categories and syntactic constructions, might conceivably be based on procedures of formal identification and classification.

Automatic translation raised the question of the mechanisation of meaning in a particularly challenging form, since the traditional view of translation was that it involved rendering an original text in one language into a second language but, as Dr Johnson's much quoted definition puts it, 'retaining the sense'. Now retaining the sense demands *prima facie* that the meaning of the text to be translated must first be understood. Could a machine understand the meaning of a text? Turing's answer, clearly, would have been that if a machine produces translations which are indistinguishable from those of a human translator, then it *has* understood what the texts mean (at least to the extent that such an understanding is necessary for purposes of translation, which is all that we demand of a human translator).

Turing's view would not have been shared by those who regarded research in automatic translation as aiming at

> a machine which, while remaining an object devoid of intelligence and of judgment, and performing a series of strictly pre-determined operations, is capable of respecting certain of the original and individual characteristics of discourse and of reproducing them faithfully in another language.[8]

But even theorists who took this more cautious view were sometimes prepared to admit that the analyses which mechanisation programmes required had the effect of

> *drawing attention to the purely mechanical character of various operatons formerly performed by a human being and accepted as mental operations.*[9]

Concessions even of this order would have attracted the critical attention of Descartes.

Again, when challenged to justify the application of the term *translation* to the process by which a punched-card tabulator

---

[8] Delavenay, op. cit., p.7.
[9] Delavenay, op. cit., p.15. (Italics in the original.)

might produce French versions of simple invoice lists in English, even a theorist of the cautious school might answer:

> But does not in fact the translator do exactly this when he renders, in a list of articles on order, *one gross fountain pens* by *12 douzaines de stylos*?[10]

The cogency of this reply depends crucially on the words 'do exactly this'. What *exactly* does the human translator *do*? Certainly not shuffle punched cards around in the cerebral cortex. Research in the field of automatic translation, as Bar-Hillel noted, was based from the outset on the assumption that since psychology could offer little but speculation as to how the human brain tackled translation, 'machine simulation of human translating' was out of the question.[11] But if this much is granted, than any assessment of the 'exactitude' with which the human translator 'does' what the tabulator does must be based on a functional rather than a physical comparison between the two. And this is the very basis of Turing's argument. Once purely functional criteria are invoked, it may seem there is nowhere to stop short of Turing's conclusion.

Those who stoutly maintained, as Colin Cherry did, that 'machine translation is of course not concerned with "meaning" at all' but merely with 'textual substitutes, from an original to a target language'[12] simply dug for themselves the pit of explaining how semantically 'blind' processes of textual substitution could somehow manage to produce translations.

Apart from refocussing attention on meaning at a period when (in American linguistics at least) 'meaning' was an altogether suspect topic best avoided, machine translation also raised theoretical questions about meaning which had never been raised before – a further demonstration of how a new look at language in a mechanical perspective could jolt established linguistic thinking out of a rut. One such question was whether the number of meanings a word had could be counted (and if so, how)? Hitherto in the Western tradition distinguishing between different lexical meanings had been left to the whim or initiative of individual lexicographers. Saussurean linguistics had simply

---

[10] Delavenay, op. cit., p.17.

[11] 'The future of machine translation', 1962. Bar-Hillel, op. cit., p.180.

[12] C.Cherry, *On Human Communication*, Cambridge, Mass. 1957, p.114.

assumed that differences in meaning were intuitively clear in particular cases, and not pressed theoretical inquiry further. Nor had Bloomfield. For the distributionalists, the question was in any case quite irrelevant. But for machine translation it became crucial, since quite different translations might be required for each separate meaning of a word.

The question of how to count meanings led directly on to one which was even more central to the concerns of linguistic theorists. How is the distinction to be drawn between a single word with two meanings and two words which share the same form? Or is there, in principle, no difference? Existing dictionaries were often guided on this point by etymological considerations. But etymologies were no help to the translator. For purposes of translation it made no difference that *bank* meaning 'river margin' and *bank* meaning 'financial institution' were etymologically of German and Romance origin respectively. That did not differentiate the case of *bank* from the case of *tank*, where two no less diverse meanings ('storage container' and 'armoured military vehicle') were associated with an etymologically unique form. Machine translation thus raised a basic semantic question about the identity of the 'word', a unit which had been taken for granted by most discussions of sentence structure for the previous two thousand years.

A related question was where exactly the boundary between syntax and semantics lay. This question had been dodged rather than solved both in traditional grammar and in modern linguistics, but it demanded a very clear answer once machines had to be equipped with precise decoding procedures. A grammar and a lexicon immediately became two mechanically separable components, but with functions which had to be co-ordinated in every detail if mistranslation were to be avoided. For example, the correct translation of the English word *sleep* is likely to depend on whether or not it occurs in the text as a 'noun' or a 'verb', to use the traditional grammatical terms. Which it is may be clear enough in certain syntactic contexts (*a long sleep* vs. *go to sleep*), but there may be others which offer no syntactic clues (*Why not sleep?*). To some extent it appears that our normal understanding of what individual words mean in texts is a matter of identifying the syntactic pattern of sentences in which they occur. On the one hand this seems to point to the conclusion that the noun *sleep* has a different meaning from the verb *sleep*. On the other hand it seems counterintuitive to deny that both the noun *sleep* and the verb *sleep* in some sense 'have the same meaning', although this is much less clear for a pair like the noun *turn* and the verb *turn* (*your turn* vs. *turn round*).

Questions of the interrelationship of grammar and semantics also extend to whole sentences. The ambiguity of the English sentence *Mary doesn't like cooking apples* depends on the fact that, to put it in traditional grammatical terminology, the gerund *cooking* and the participial or adjectival *cooking* are morphologically identical, and this holds not only for the verb *cook* but for all English verbs. If *Mary doesn't like cooking apples* is taken in one sense, it follows that there are some kinds of apple that Mary does not like; whereas if it is taken in the other sense that does not follow at all. But these semantic differences cannot be plausibly explained by supposing that English has two verbs *cook* with different meanings. Somehow a translation machine has to be provided with the means of detecting systematic syntactic subtleties of this kind, and supplying an appropriate translation in each case.

How grammatical distinctions and semantic distinctions intermesh was to become a controversial topic in linguistic theory, particularly with the advent of transformational grammar, which is itself ushered in with the gypsy's warning that 'there is no aspect of linguistic study more subject to confusion'.[13] The subsequent history of the transformational controversy had little if anything to do with problems in translation, but the form which the controversy took owed a great deal to the emergence in machine translation of an option between one or other of two general strategies. One strategy was to treat semantics as a residuum of problems left over after grammatical analysis was completed. The other strategy was exactly the opposite: to leave grammar as a residuum of problems which could not be dealt with in terms of the meanings of individual forms. The latter translation strategy could be seen as 'starting from the idea that syntax was of minor importance in the understanding of a language'.[14] Transformationalists, on the contrary, were to maximise the importance of syntax, and to advance the quite novel claim that 'in order to understand a

[13] Chomsky, op. cit., p.93.
[14] Delavenay, op. cit., p.34.

sentence it is necessary to know the kernel sentences from which it originates (more precisely the terminal strings underlying these kernel sentences) and the phrase structure of each of these elementary components, as well as the transformational history of development of the given sentence from these kernel sentences'.[15] Thus a large part of 'understanding' is reduced to grasping purely mechanical processes underlying – or rather constituting – syntactic structure. These processes are regarded as intrinsically meaningless. The notion that they have some kind of 'structural meaning' is dismissed as being quite 'suspect', and it is held to be 'questionable that the grammatical devices available in language are used consistently enough so that meaning can be assigned to them directly'.[16]

In spite of the recognition by researchers in machine translation that there were formidable problems to be overcome, confidence in the ultimate feasibility of the mechanisation of meaning was sustained by awareness of the progress that had already been achieved in logic. Automata theory and mathematical logic were acknowledged as the cornerstones of cybernetics.[17] The decisive link between mathematical logic and linguistics was seen as having been forged by Post's success 'in formally assimilating rules of formation to rules of deduction, thereby paving the way for the application of the recently developed powerful theory of recursive functions... to all ordinary languages viewed as combinatorial systems'.[18] The key to mechanisation, evidently, was formalisation. Anything that could be formalised with sufficient precision could be handled by a machine. Arithmetic had already yielded. Logic was yielding.[19] Why not linguistic meaning?

As an illustration of the extent to which machines could cope with problems of meaning by 1959, Delavenay was able to include the following sample from his own book on machine translation, rendered into English by a programme designed to deal with texts on chemistry and nuclear energy.

---

[15] Chomsky, op. cit., p.92.
[16] Chomsky, op. cit., p.108.
[17] N.Wiener, *Cybernetics*, New York 1948.
[18] Bar-Hillel, op. cit., p.186.
[19] By 1956 Newell and Simon's 'Logic Theorist' program had produced on a computer the first complete proof of a theorem from Whitehead and Russell's *Principia Mathematica*.

AVANT – PROPOS
PRE1SENTER AU LECTEUR QUI N EST SPE1CIALISE1 NI DANS
L E1TUDE DE LA LINGUISTIQUE NI DANS LA CONNAISSANCE
DES CALCULATRICES E1LECTRONIQUES, LES PROBLE2MES
ACTUELS DE LA TRADUCTION AUTOMATIQUE DES LANGUES,
TEL EST LE BUT DANS LEQUEL CE LIVRE A E1TE1 CONCU.

BEFORE – REMARK
TO PRESENT AT THE READER WHICH IS SPE1CIALISED
NEITHER IN THE STUDY OF THE LINGUISTIC NOR IN THE
KNOWLEDGE OF THE ELECTRONIC CALCULATRICES, THE
PRESENT PROBLEMS OF THE AUTOMATIC TRADUCTION OF
THE LANGUES, SUCH IS THE AIM IN WHICH THIS BOOK HAS
BEEN CONCEIVED.

Apart from the superficial oddities consequent upon
representing acute and grave accents orthographically as Arabic
numerals, the English version reads remarkably like the effort of
a French beginner struggling to master English in the early
stages of learning that language. It would be a fortunate teacher
who could honestly claim never to have come across such a bad
translation in the exercises or examination papers submitted by
pupils learning a foreign language. It would, moreover, be a
Draconian teacher who gave such a translation no marks at all.
Judged by this evidence, the translation machine would appear
to be at least within striking distance of passing the Turing test.
That is, there is a class of human (admittedly inferior)
translators with whom the machine might compete at a level
which would make it quite difficult for an investigator to detect
the machine. Anyone willing to concede this much, if only for the
sake of argument, has *ipso facto* conceded that it makes sense to
conceptualise at least some semantic skills by reference to the
comparative achievements of humans and machines. It is in this
sense that the automatic translation programme of the postwar
period, however limited its successes may have been in practice,
marks a significant conceptual advance in establishing the
mythology of the language machine.

In some ways, the gap between what translation machines
could achieve and what human translators could achieve dealt
an even more devastating blow to doubts about the mechanisation of meaning than if there had been no gap at all. For the

superiority of the human translator over the machine turned out to be principally in tidying up minor, relatively marginal linguistic details, and *not* in the core task of analysing the 'source language' text and substituting verbal equivalents in the 'target language'. Thus it became possible to envisage as a practical proposition a 'collaboration' between the human translator and the machine, by which the human being would merely hand-finish and polish a rough-and-ready textual product delivered by machine processing. (The human polishing was known technically as 'post-editing'.)

If semantic equivalences are central to translation, then even on the most sceptical interpretation, the consequences of the demonstration that machines can process texts so as to produce what human beings regard as translations of them must have far-reaching implications for our understanding of linguistic meaning. The question is neither whether the translation machine is a 'fraud' because it merely 'mimics' understanding, nor whether the term *translation machine* itself is a misdescription; but how it is possible for human translators themselves to build machines which can successfully replicate results seemingly dependent on the application of semantic knowledge. Even if the sceptic still denies that the machine can in any sense understand the texts it translates, it becomes foolish any longer to deny that the aid of such a machine can make it possible systematically to convert a text in one language into another language, both the original text and the conversion being independently understandable by human beings, and recognised by bilinguals as communicationally equivalent to at least a significant degree of approximation. At the very minimum, then, the machine can broaden the linguistic horizons of its monoglot human user, by affording access of some kind to languages the monoglot human does not know. That in itself forces one to ask on what semantic principles the machine's success is based, and how the implementation of these principles *makes* the machine work. This is a different matter altogether from asking for a description of the machine's operations, which may be quite unenlightening. Rather, it is a question analogous to that which forces itself on the attention of anyone who discovers that with the aid of a telescope it becomes possible to see objects invisible to the naked eye. Somehow, it is clear, the principles implemented (whether accidentally or deliberately) in the construction of the telescope make an 'extension' of human sight possible. We do not have to suppose that the telescope itself 'sees' the object and then passes on what it sees to the human eye. At the same time, we realise that anyone unacquainted with telescopes who thought it out of the question for a man-made contrivance to extend our range of vision cannot fully have understood how the human eye works. To that extent, the invention of the telescope places a permanent restriction on plausible theories of the eye. By the same token, it becomes clear that it will not do to explain away the translation machine by saying simply that it works by implementing a crude version of the principles involved in human translation. That would only be admissible if we already knew how the human translator works. Analogously, it would not do to explain away the telescope by saying that it works on much the same principles as the eye, unless we already had an adequate understanding of human optics.

If the automatic translation programme of the post-war period ultimately proved to be a disappointment, it was not because its best machines were not as good as had been expected, but because of a failure to press hard enough the theoretical question of why they were as good as they were. That was not, however, the reason usually given. By 1960 Bar-Hillel, 'the first full-time paid research worker' in the field of automatic translation, had in practice abandoned his earlier optimistic conviction that 'if a human being can do it, a suitably programmed computer can do it too'.[20] He had come to the opposite view that it was possible to give 'an almost full-fledged demonstration' that fully automatic high quality translation (that is, of a quality indistinguishable from human translation) was unattainable 'not only in the near future but altogether'.[21] The demonstration he gives is one of the most interesting documents in the history of the subject. What it demonstrates is not what Bar-Hillel claims, but rather that the myth of the language machine, once accepted, leads straight to a 'mechanisation paradox' in semantics.

Bar-Hillel begins his demonstration by attacking what he calls

[20] Bar-Hillel, op. cit., p.9. Curiously, he still maintained that this was correct 'in principle', while offering no reason for believing so, and claiming to have shown that otherwise than 'in principle' it was false.
[21] 'Aims and Methods in Machine Translation', 1960. Bar-Hillel, op. cit., p.167.

the 'prejudice' in automatic translation research that semantic ambiguities can be resolved mechanically by programming a machine to scan a sufficiently extensive section of the verbal context in which the semantically ambiguous word occurs. This 'prejudice' leads to the notion that the only practical problem to be solved is that of the minimum value of N, where N is the number of words to be scanned on either side of the ambiguous word. Bar-Hillel argues that the 'fateful fallacy' in this is that while it may be valid for 'intelligent readers', it is not valid for electronic computers, even if they are powerful enough to scan whole paragraphs or whole books. Bar-Hillel gives as an example the sentence *The box was in the pen*. The context in which this sentence occurs in the text to be translated is as follows: *Little John was looking for his toy box. Finally he found it. The box was in the pen. John was very happy.* The semantic ambiguity involved is assumed to be that the word *pen* might here have either of two meanings: (i) 'writing implement', or (ii) 'playpen'. According to Bar-Hillel 'no existing or imaginable program will enable an electronic computer to determine that the word *pen* in the given sentence in the given context has the second of the above meanings, whereas every reader with a sufficient knowledge of English will do this "automatically".' The final word in the previous sentence and its scare quotes already point to the dilemma in which Bar-Hillel finds himself.

Bar-Hillel wishes to argue that the reason why the human being here can outperform any 'existing or imaginable' computer program is that the human being has available a certain item of knowledge:

> that the relative sizes of pens, in the sense of writing implements, toy boxes, and pens, in the sense of playpens, are such that when someone writes under ordinary circumstances and in something like the given context, 'The box was in the pen,' he almost certainly refers to a playpen and most certainly not to a writing pen.... This knowledge is not at the disposal of the electronic computer and none of the dictionaries or programs for the elimination of polysemy puts this knowledge at its disposal.

This, *prima facie*, is a quite astonishing reason to advance, given that we are considering all computer programs 'existing or imaginable'; and Bar-Hillel proceeds immediately to counter the obvious objection that there is no hindrance to imagining a program which *does* put this knowledge at the disposal of the machine.

The objection will not hold, says Bar-Hillel, because it entails the requirement that the translation machine should have available not only a dictionary but also a 'universal encyclopedia'. And the reason why this is impracticable is that the 'encyclopedia' of facts which human beings know is infinite.

Infinity is the big stick one sees wielded time and again in post-war controversies over language. It has come to replace appeals to divine authority. But the interesting point about using it to 'demonstrate' the futility of any attempt at mechanical resolution of problems of semantic ambiguity is that its use in that context merely makes the explanatory dilemma more acute. Clearly, any computer program *could* incorporate the specific item of information which *ex hypothesi* is needed for the mechanical disambiguation of the word *pen* in the context envisaged. That particular program would then have solved that particular problem. But, so the argument runs, no single program could incorporate *all* such items of information, because they are infinite in number. So total mechanisation of all information is simultaneously the only solution and an impossible solution.

As an example of self-defeating ingenuity this argument could hardly be bettered. For it applies *pari passu* to the human translator, whose semantic skill the machine allegedly cannot match. Any *particular* human translator who happened to be ignorant of some particular fact relevant to the material to be translated would presumably, in the absence of contextual clues, get caught out by verbal ambiguity which turned precisely on that item of information. But presumably no single human being has access to all human knowledge. It would be absurd to conclude from this that human translators have not yet discovered the right way to translate, and even more absurd to conclude that what was hampering them was the infinity of items of information which might turn out to be relevant to an imaginary totality of texts.

*   *   *

Transformationalists of the early 1960s were already writing off machine translation on the ground that it had 'scarcely contributed any basic insights into linguistic structure'.[22] What this really meant was that linguistic theory had now caught up with translation theory and become even more fundamentally machine-oriented.

When the 'behaviourist period' in American linguistics was officially declared closed,[23] there followed the reinstatement of meaning as a legitimate and fruitful topic of general linguistic inquiry. The price of reinstatement, however, was that the central problems of semantics were then dealt with as purely mechanical problems, on all fours with the corresponding problems of syntax. Thus Bloomfield's 'mechanistic' approach was repudiated, only to be replaced by a linguistics no less mechanistic in spirit than the most committed Bloomfieldian could have wished.

What emerged as the approved transformational-generative doctrine of meaning took as its basic premiss that 'linguistic description minus grammar equals semantics'.[24] In other words, semantics was residual. The strategy advocated was 'to determine, when we have subtracted the problems in the description of a language properly belonging to grammar, what problems belong to semantics'.[25] The residual nature of these problems meant, predictably, that they would be identified by reference to an already established mechanical model of syntax. The earlier treatment of speakers as 'syntax machines' prefigured their eventual treatment as 'meaning machines' too. It is perhaps worth emphasising the inevitability of this development: for unless semantics is to be considered as entirely unrelated to syntax, once syntax is conceptualised in terms of the operations of a machine the internal logic of linguistic description demands a parallel treatment for semantics. More specifically, given a device which generates all and only the grammatical sentences of a language, the natural way to develop semantics is either to ask what limitations have to be placed on this device in order to ensure that it generates all and only

[22] E.Bach, *An Introduction to Transformational Grammars*, New York 1964, p.144.

[23] By Chomsky's polemically anti-behaviourist review of B.F.Skinner's book *Verbal Behavior*, published in *Language*, vol.35, 1959.

[24] J.J.Katz and J.A.Fodor, 'The structure of a semantic theory', *Language*, vol.39, 1963. Reprinted in J.A.Fodor and J.J.Katz (eds.), *The Structure of Language*, Englewood Cliffs 1964. Page references are to the reprint.

[25] Katz and Fodor, op. cit., p.483.

sentences which are *both* grammatical *and* semantically impeccable, or else to ask what further device will accept as input all the grammatical sentences and weed out those which are semantically deviant (nonsensical).

Katz and Fodor develop their semantic argument by considering a meaning machine which is limited to analysing English sentences on the basis of the information supplied in an English dictionary. The machine, it is assumed, can find the relevant dictionary entry for any given morpheme in any given sentence. The problem, as Katz and Fodor see it, is that this machine 'will not be able to select the sense(s) the morpheme actually bears in a given sentential context, except insofar as the selection is already determined by the grammatical markers assigned to the morpheme in the derivation of the sentence'.[26] Thus, given a sentence like *One of the oil seals in my car is leaking*, the machine will be unable to determine the appropriate sense of the noun *seal* in view of the fact that the dictionary entry lists several meanings for this noun.

> What the machine is failing to do is take account of or utilise the semantic relations between morphemes in a sentence. Thus, the machine cannot determine the correct number and content of readings of a sentence; nor can it distinguish semantically anomalous sentences from semantically regular ones.[27]

Katz and Fodor's (strange) assumption seems to be that the reason why the human reader or hearer of the sentence *One of the oil seals in my car is leaking* is not misled into thinking that the seals in question are marine animals or pieces of stamped wax is that the human being, unlike the machine, knows the semantic relations in English between the morphemes *oil* and *seal* (and possibly *car* and *leak* as well).

The implications of this example are clear. If the machine *could* be allowed access to information about the semantic relations between morphemes in a sentence, and could utilise this information to determine 'correct' readings, discard semantically anomalous sentences, identify paraphrases, etc., then it would match the semantic ability of a fluent speaker of English. The solution Katz and Fodor propose is to supply every

[26] Katz and Fodor, op. cit., p.492.
[27] Katz and Fodor, op. cit., p.493.

entry in the dictionary component with 'semantic markers' (such as *Human, Animal, Male*) and then set up a 'projection rule component' which is organised so as to permit certain combinations of semantic markers and prohibit others. The outcome of all this apparatus is a 'semantic component' which can assign to all sentences their 'correct' possible readings, resolve ambiguities (where they can be resolved) and detect anomalies, paraphrases and tautologies. The exact details of the apparatus are of no particular relevance here, except to note that what is proposed is in effect an input-output device which applies combinatorial rules to the sequences of units it is processing.

One obvious objection to a 'meaning machine' of this design is that it will be unable to deal with examples like Bar-Hillel's *The box was in the pen*. Or rather, it will only be able to do so on condition that (i) the machine be allowed to take account of the semantic relations between morphemes occurring not only in the same sentence but in neighbouring sentences, and (ii) the dictionary entries to which the machine has access contain the relevant information about the relative sizes of writing implements, toy boxes and playpens. Katz and Fodor evidently foresee the likelihood of an objection along these lines, and make two moves to forestall it. One is to point out that 'except for a few types of cases, discourse can be treated as a single sentence in isolation by regarding sentence boundaries as sentential connectives'.[28] But this move will be of no avail in Bar-Hillel's example, since even if the four relevant sentences are collapsed into, for instance, *Little John, looking for his toy box, finally found it in the pen and was very happy* this still leaves the ambiguity of *pen* unresolved. Katz and Fodor's second move is more Olympian. It is to draw an absolute distinction between 'knowledge of a language' and 'knowledge of the world', and to deny that semantics is concerned with the latter. This move, clearly, leaves ample room to dismiss any awkward case like *the box was in the pen* on the ground that knowledge of the relative sizes of writing implements, playpens, etc., is 'knowledge of the world', and therefore falls outside the scope of a semantic theory.

What is of interest in the present context is not so much the complete silence Katz and Fodor maintain on the subject of how

[28] Katz and Fodor, op. cit., p.490.

exactly it will ever be possible to draw a clear distinction between 'knowledge of the language' and 'knowledge of the world' for all particular instances, but the reason they offer for insisting that somehow or other such a distinction must be drawn. Their reason is that, for *practically any item of information about the world*, it is possible to construct a sentence containing an ambiguity which cannot be resolved except on the basis of knowing that particular item of information. In other words, the knowledge required to resolve all such ambiguities would be infinite. But this is just the reason Bar-Hillel gave for denying that there is any mechanical solution to the problem of resolving the textual ambiguities which 'every reader with a sufficient knowledge of English' can resolve 'automatically'. Katz and Fodor appeal to the same consideration in order to restrict the domain of English semantic knowledge to tasks which their apparatus of markers and projection rules can handle. In both cases, the motive is the same. The exclusion of the infinity of items of information which speakers may in practice take into account in understanding what they read or hear is the only way to ensure that the theoretical world of semantics can be ruled by the meaning machine.

Thus by 1963 not only had the familiar descriptive techniques of mechanisation infiltrated the last remaining area of language study, but linguistic theorists were threatening that unless they were allowed to restrict 'knowledge of meanings' to the kind of information machines could handle, it would be impossible to develop any 'serious' account of the semantics of natural languages (as distinct from formal or artificial languages) at all. The myth of the language machine had finally been transformed into science.

Part II

The Machine Without

Die Sprache ist die Maschine

Die Bewegung des Maschinensymbols ist in andere Weise
vorausbestimmt, als die einer gegebenen wirklichen Maschine

Wittgenstein

Chapter Five
The Grammarians' Paradise

When a few years ago a computer scientist asked 'What is it about the computer that has brought the view of man as a machine to a new level of plausibility?'[1] he was putting the question the wrong way round. It should have been 'What is it about the view of man as a machine that has brought the computer to a new level of plausibility?' The answer has already been sketched in the preceding chapters. La Mettrie's theory of *l'homme machine* lacked any detailed account of how the human capacity for language could credibly be described as simply 'mechanical'. The language machine remained a metaphor until Saussure. Only then did linguists begin to envisage linguistics as dealing with the analysis of a working *mécanisme de la langue* housed in the human brain. When the computer eventually showed itself to be on the way to handling language as competently as the human brain, its intellectual status began to rise. It was already presenting its credentials to be recognised as a potential life-form.

A bare outline of the story of the language machine from its pre-Cartesian beginnings to its post-Saussurean culmination risks giving the impression that we are dealing merely with 'history of ideas' in the shallowest sense: that is, with the influence of a few dominant individual thinkers upon a rather small, donnish coterie of academics and intellectuals. Even greater, perhaps, is the risk that the technological side of the story from Pascal down to PASCAL, apparently written by mathematically minded boffins and wizards of the electronics laboratory, will assume predominant importance. Nothing could be further from the truth. We shall have failed to understand the

---

[1] J.Weizenbaum, *Computer Power and Human Reason*, San Francisco 1976, p.8.

story of the language machine altogether unless we read it as a narrative whose articulation reflects an underlying social transformation, and see that its shape is determined by what was probably the most momentous development in the social history of modern Europe: the introduction of universal education.

The equation 'man = machine' had long been preceded by the equation 'machine = slave'. In Europe, that earlier equation sprang from social conditions already established in the civilisations of Greece and Rome. The social history of Western technology is largely the history of replacing slaves by machines, machines being on the whole more efficient, more docile and less expensive. When the mechanisation of cotton picking in the USA in the 1930s handed over to machines a form of labour traditionally the occupation of slaves, it merely repeated the economic lesson already taught in Gaul in the fourth century by the Roman engineer who demonstrated that a stepped series of water-powered millstones could grind more flour in a day than rotary quern grinding by slave labour could produce in a month. (It is worth noting that the slaves, both in the Graeco-Roman world and in the cotton fields of America, had originally been captives from foreign lands, and hence not members of the linguistic community.) The present-day replacement of factory workers by robots continues essentially the same trend. The robots raise output, cut costs, and will not go on strike; and the etymology of the word *robot* itself perpetuates the association between automation and slavery.

So there was never any objection to an equation between the human and the mechanical in the Western tradition, as long as it was understood that the human side of the equation applied only to members of one (socially inferior) class of human beings, and that the comparison related to the execution of tasks under the direction of a master. The fundamental analogy between the function of a slave and the function of a machine was ultimately based on ownership. It was ownership which conferred the right to use both slaves and machines, to profit from the work done by both, and to determine the treatment accorded to them. Thus 'machine = slave' is the reflection of a pattern of social control and of the exercise of authority derived from an established social structure. The later equation 'man = machine' is likewise the reflection of a pattern of social control, and of the exercise of authority, although of a more subtle kind.

These equations also reach a deeper level. Just as slavery is a paradigm of control over human beings, machinery is a paradigm of control over Nature. By means of machines, from the invention of the six 'simple machines'[2] onwards, it was possible to exploit natural mechanical principles in order to overcome natural obstacles. Slavery was the parallel exploitation of elementary psychological principles (fear of pain, hunger, etc., hope of freedom) to harness human labour. It is clear, however, that it took a very long time for our ancestors, even having reached a relatively advanced stage of civilisation in social and material terms, to appreciate the fundamental difference between physical and psychological phenomena.[3] Hence the ubiquity of animistic explanations for natural processes and events, attested in primitive mythology the world over. The original archetype of orderliness was a social archetype, not one derived from observation of the natural scene.

How compelling the archetype of social order was as the mould of explanatory thinking is clear from the early conceptualisation of divinities as law-givers. Divine law could be envisaged as encompassing not only human conduct, but all forms of life and the inanimate world as well, particularly if the divinity in question was also conceived of as the original maker of the universe. Thus the notion of obedience (to divine law) could unproblematically span everything from morality to meteorology. The supreme attribute of the divinity, according to this conceptual scheme, is *auctoritas*, that authority which combines the power of creation with the power of commanding obedience. The divinity becomes the author of universal order in both capacities. The assumption of divine authority by kings, needless to say, was always rooted more firmly in their efficacy as regulators of the social order than in their ability to move mountains, which must always have seemed limited and dubious even to the most obedient of subjects.

The persistence of social order as an explanatory archetype into a later era is strikingly attested by the metaphor of 'laws of Nature', as Jonathan Miller points out:

---

[2] Traditionally regarded as being the lever, the screw, the wheel and axle, the pulley, the inclined plane and the wedge (the last two sometimes treated as variants of a single device).

[3] R.L.Gregory, *Mind in Science*, London 1981, Ch.1.

By systematically cultivating their status as human beings, men acquired such confidence in their own prudent nobility that they were no longer overawed by the competing majesty of nature. Far from *eclipsing* scientific curiosity, the image of civic order celebrated under the humanist regime could confront nature as an orderly and explicable entity. If human affairs yielded so gracefully to decency and decorum why shouldn't nature conform to the same benevolent plan? It is not an accident that the regularities of the cosmos should have been christened with the title 'Law'.[4]

By the nineteenth century this had become a second-generation metaphor (or 'metametaphor'). The idea that the physical universe had its own 'laws' was in turn extended to psychological phenomena. Thus George Boole could claim, on the basis of purely logical analysis, to have uncovered the 'laws of thought'. According to Boole, these laws of thought could provide the basis for a 'philosophical language',[5] an ideal which had been conjured up repeatedly in philosophical and scientific circles for the past two hundred years. At the same time as Boole was investigating these 'laws of thought', linguists claimed to be revealing laws of language, both physiological (i.e. relating to sound change) and psychological (i.e. relating to meanings). In virtually every field of academic inquiry by the end of the century, the detection of patterns of any kind was being proclaimed as the discovery of 'laws'. What had begun as a potent and persuasive analogy ended in trivialisation.

This trivialisation is of pivotal significance for the human sciences in general, for it tends to blur the difference between rules and regularities (both subsumable under 'laws'). Nowhere is this difference more important than in relation to language, where the priority of rules over mere regularities is the conceptual cornerstone of the entire Western tradition of grammatical studies.

* * *

The term *rule* as applied to language is perhaps most familiar in the traditional expression *rule of grammar*. But exactly what a rule is in this sense seems to be not altogether clear; at least, if

[4] J.Miller, *McLuhan*, London 1971, p.56. For other possible explanations, see J.E.Ruby, 'The Origins of Scientific "Law" ', *Journal of the History of Ideas*, vol.47, 1986.
[5] G.Boole, *The Mathematical Analysis of Logic*, Cambridge 1847.

we are to judge by a passage such as the following from a recently
published manual of the Cree language, the most widely spoken
of the Algonquian languages of Canada:

> In all languages there are so-called 'rules of grammar'. These
> rules should not be regarded as arbitrary laws which the language
> *must* obey, but rather as a set of systematized observations on the
> way the signal code appears to function. In this sense,
> grammatical rules are like the 'laws' of nature, they reflect our
> understanding of the system as far as we have been able to discern
> it.[6]

This comment prefaces a note on certain apparent 'illogicalities'
in the way Cree sentences are constructed. The note concludes
by advising would-be learners of Cree that when they hear an
expression which they have difficulty fitting into a grammatical
pattern, they should simply learn how and where to use it and
'worry later about the logic involved, if any'. This advice is
preceded by a quotation from one of the most distinguished
scholars in the field of Amerindian languages, Edward Sapir:

> The fact of grammar, a universal trait of language, is simply a
> generalized expression of the feeling that analogous concepts and
> relations are most conveniently symbolized in analogous forms.
> Were a language ever completely 'grammatical' it would be a
> perfect engine of conceptual expression. Unfortunately, or luckily,
> no language is tyrannically consistent. All grammars leak.[7]

Cree grammar, it appears, is particularly leaky.

The two paragraphs just quoted manage between them to
invoke a whole range of figurative comparisons which cluster
round the notions of order, authority and machinery.
Disconcertingly, these comparisons crisscross in a way which, far
from clarifying for the reader what grammar is, leave it as a
puzzle. The reference to 'so-called "rules of grammar" ', with its
scare quotes, perhaps suggests that these so-called rules are not
really rules at all. At the end we still do not know how grammar
is instituted and promulgated, or indeed changed; nor by whom.
Whereas the notion of authority appeared to invite such
questions, bringing in the notions of natural law and machinery

---

[6] C.D.Ellis, *Spoken Cree*, 2nd ed., Edmonton, Alberta 1983, p.257.
[7] E.Sapir, *Language*, New York 1921, p.39.

discourages them. Or perhaps we are prompted to ask instead who designed this defective 'engine' with its irregularities of morphology and syntax, from which grammar 'leaks' like the oil drips from botched joints or badly aligned connexions. Why don't all the parts fit together? Does Nature tolerate mechanical imperfection? Does the universe leak as well?

These conundrums pile up on a single page of a scholarly work devoted to a cause which will nowadays strike many as academically Quixotic: the teaching of a language which must by any reckoning be doomed to extinction in the not too distant future. The historical irony pervading the author's discussion of Cree grammar is its failure to mention the most pertinent sense of the term *grammar* at all: the sense in which grammar arrived on the scene too late to save the Cree language. This is also the sense in which the Cree people had no grammar until the arrival of the white man in North America. *Ave grammatica, morituri te salutant.*

Grammar in this primary sense is a European cultural product. It is also one of Europe's most successful cultural exports. Grammar is essentially concerned with literacy, of which it is the educational instrument, designed by professional educators. Grammar, in short, is the creation of grammarians.

Sociolinguists have only belatedly begun to realise that grammar as a cultural export can just as easily kill off linguistic varieties as preserve them. As Peter Mühlhäusler points out in a recent paper on 'The politics of small languages in Australia and the Pacific',[8] there is evidence that the arrival of foreign missionaries and teachers who took it upon themselves to codify in European fashion the grammar of pre-literate peoples may in many instances have constituted a disruptive intrusion into the local linguistic ecology. For, as in Europe, the selection and promotion of one particular linguistic variety confers upon it advantages which then unavoidably militate against competing varieties. As a result, linguistic varieties may well disappear which would have survived but for the (doubtless well intentioned) efforts of the grammarian.

The educational role of the grammarian was first established in the Graeco-Roman world, where grammar was recognised as one of three language-related studies (the other two being logic

---

[8] *Language & Communication*, vol.7, 1987.

and rhetoric).[9] In virtue of their educational role, grammarians collectively may be seen as accredited public custodians of the nation's language. By teaching it to the young they assume collective responsibility for passing on the language from one generation to the next. Inevitably, given that the only Graeco-Roman concept of education was preceptive, grammar, like all other educational subjects, had to have precepts. Consequently the grammarians exercised their collective custodianship of the nation's language in practice by formulating linguistic rules. The formulation of such rules was pedagogically essential to the grammarian's function in the educational system to which grammar belonged.

As a result, grammar as a cultural product had built in from the start three assumptions about language which have their *raison d'être* in a specific educational curriculum and a preferred method of teaching it. This fact was to have incalculable consequences for the subsequent history of linguistics and for the Western view of mental phenomena in general. One was the assumption that language needs a model, paragon or exemplar in order to function at all. The second was that (even imperfect) approximation to such a model, paragon, or exemplar is what constitutes mastery of a language, and simultaneously provides the criteria for judging particular instances of linguistic usage. The third was that the desired approximation is, at least for the general run of mortals, to be achieved by somehow learning rules.

Grammar thus taught promulgates a plainly authoritarian concept of language. That all three assumptions are, to say the least, dubious never apparently occurred to any Classical grammarian; and if it had, the doubt would have been prejudicial if not outright disastrous to a successful career. In the annals of grammar we have to wait until we reach the calculated, deliberately decadent scepticism of the post-Classical period before we find any attempt to pull the educational carpet from under the grammarians' feet. Sextus Empiricus is the first hippy in the history of linguistics. Like most hippies, he was too *outré* to be effective. By then, in any case, the grammatical establishment could afford to ignore him.

The basic problem for the orthodox grammarian was that only

[9] R.Harris, *The Language-Makers*, London 1980, Chs.4 and 5.

part of the curriculum lent itself to being taught by means of rules. We can observe this as a recurrent educational tension throughout the entire history of Western literacy. It surfaces time and again. One of its conspicuous manifestations in twentieth-century academia is the split in university 'language' departments between 'linguistic' (including 'philological') studies and the study of 'literature'. Since the analysis of particular literary works is not amenable to preceptive statement, the trend which inevitably emerges in opposition to the preceptive approach is seen, as E.M.W.Tillyard once said of the Cambridge English school, as a trend 'towards gossipy, and often highly metaphorical, description and unspecific praise'.[10] Praise, because unless the texts were praiseworthy they presumably would not have been prescribed for study in the first place.

In Graeco-Roman education it was assumed without question that only certain types of text were praiseworthy.This is already reflected in Dionysius Thrax's epochal definition of grammar as 'the practical knowledge of the general usages of poets and prose writers'.[11] This definition is geared to a particular culture in a particular phase of social development. It could hardly apply to civilisations which had neither poetry nor prose. More generally, it could hardly apply to civilisations without writing. Dionysius' specification of the six parts of grammar makes it clear that the whole programme presupposes literacy. The six parts are:

> first, accurate reading (aloud) with due regard to the prosodies; second, explanation of the literary expressions in the works; third, the provision of notes on phraseology and subject matter; fourth, the discovery of etymologies; fifth, the working out of analogical regularities; sixth, the appreciation of literary compositions, which is the noblest part of grammar.[12]

The programme as Dionysius gives it is a somewhat

[10] E.M.W.Tillyard, *The Muse Unchained*, London 1958, p.84.
  The same split was a live issue when the Oxford English school was founded and Churton Collins attacked philology as 'a wretched system of word-mongering'. Cf.D.J.Palmer, *The Rise of English Studies*, Oxford 1965, Chs. 6-7.
  [11] R.H.Robins, *A Short History of Linguistics*, 2nd ed., London, p.31. The attribution of the much quoted *Techne Grammatike* to the historical Dionysius of the second century B.C. is questionable. It may well be a compilation of a much later period.
  [12] Robins, loc. cit.

unconvincing hotchpotch. Some parts have obvious practical applications, while others apparently have none. What use could the discovery of etymologies be to the average pupil? (Archbishop Trench[13] had an answer to this in the nineteenth century; but almost certainly the archbishop's answer, which involved inculcating national pride and revealing the hand of God in all things, would not have appealed to etymologists of Dionysius' day.)

Commenting on Dionysius' curriculum, R.H.Robins points out that 'only the fifth division, the working out of regularities in the language, or of analogy, covers both what then and later was regarded as the central province of grammar, and this is the only division that actually receives detailed development in the text.'[14] One might add that it seems significant that only this division and the first cover matters which are obviously amenable to the formulation of rules.

Quintilian in the first century A.D. gives a rather different account of what the *grammaticus* was supposed to teach. Grammar, according to Quintilian, divides into just two parts: *scientia recte loquendi* (which deals with correct speech) and *enarratio poetarum* (which deals with literary texts).[15] The former patently lends itself more readily to setting up rules than the latter, and it seems clear both from Quintilian's description and from Priscian's *Partitiones*[16] that rule-based exercises must in practice have been the core of grammatical instruction in the classroom.

Robins observes that what lies behind Dionysius' fifth division of grammar is the long-standing conflict between two views about Greek: the analogist view and the anomalist view. Partisans of the former held the Greek language to be an orderly, rational system, while partisans of the latter stressed on the contrary the many irregularities and inconsistencies of Greek. The Alexandrian school, to which Dionysius Thrax belonged, favoured the analogist view. 'The first extant formulation of Greek grammar, and the pattern for centuries of later work can thus be seen as a product of the analogist-anomalist argument.'[17] For two thousand

---

[13] *On The Study of Words*, London 1851.

[14] Robins, loc. cit.

[15] *Institutio Oratoria* I, iv, 2.

[16] R.Harris, op. cit., p.106f.

[17] Robins, loc. cit. Arguably, this also explains Dionysius' inclusion of 'the discovery of etymologies', which are likely to reveal original analogical patterns later obscured.

years, in fact, the analogists swept all before them. Sapir's dictum that 'all grammars leak' is no more than a belated Parthian shot fired by a retreating anomalist in full flight.

Grammar as institutionalised in European education thus represents simultaneously a triumph for an analogist view of language and for an authoritarian view of language. There is no reason why the two should necessarily go together. Hence it is all the more important to realise that in this particular historical instance they do, and that the connexion has a purely pedagogic rather than a theoretical basis. The analogist position naturally commends itself to the grammarian in the classroom because the alternative position, anomalism, consorts ill with rule-based teaching. (For the out-and-out anomalist, presumably, morphological and syntactic patterning would have to be regarded as merely fortuitous.) Likewise, the authoritarian view also has intrinsic pedagogic advantages, not the least of which is that of having an approved corpus of texts to supply a rich fund of *exempla*.

In the Western tradition this combination of authoritarian and analogist views soon hardened into a rigid orthological dogma,[18] of which the main features are quite predictable given the initial assumptions. A principal feature of the dogma is that linguistic change is wrong. (This survives into the nineteenth and twentieth centuries in various forms, including the strongly held view that phonetic evolution is caused by laziness, slovenliness, declining standards, etc.[19]) Another is that the written form of a language is its ideal form, and that speech should accordingly conform to orthography. Another is that what confers 'correctness' on usage is either attestation in the published works of those authors set up as paragons, or else accordance with the rules which grammarians have derived from those works. Finally, it is a feature of the dogma that deviation from correctness as defined above is due to 'ignorance' (that is, lack of education and specifically illiteracy).

This was to have profound sociolinguistic implications throughout the following centuries, when not only was the great

---

[18] R.Harris, op. cit., pp.7f, 105-7, 131-2, 149, 167.

[19] As late as 1949 one finds that in a presidential address to the English Association on 'Thought and Language' the Romance languages are referred to as 'degenerate forms of Latin' (L.S.Amery, *Thought and Language*, Oxford, 1949, p.11.)

majority of the population of Europe illiterate but virtually the only access to literacy was through an educational system controlled by the church. Thus it came about that Europe inherited from antiquity a concept of language by which the illiterate were in effect linguistically disfranchised. If they happened sometimes to speak 'grammatically' that could only be by good luck, or through slavish but uncomprehending imitation of their betters. They could not follow rules of grammar (*grammatice loqui*) because, being uneducated, they had no means of knowing what the rules of grammar were.

Perhaps most important of all, the notion of using a language 'grammatically' could in any case apply only to those languages which had grammatical rules. These languages were, in the first instance and for a long time, just Greek and Latin. Other languages, it was held, were not yet 'fixed': which meant that no grammarian had done for them what the grammarians of Greece and Rome had done for Greek and Latin - lay down the rules. A language not 'fixed' was a mere vernacular or pot-pourri of dialects, good enough for peasants or merchants but not fit for more exalted purposes. Hence the importance eventually attached by all the emergent nations of post-medieval Europe to having their national language duly codified by grammarians. That grammatical imprimatur set the seal on their status as 'civilised' countries.

Thus the permanent social basis for the authoritarian concept of language which became established in the Western tradition was a longstanding professional alliance between two influential minorities, the grammarians and the writers, both groups belonging to an educational élite. It was in the interests of both to inculcate a concern for adherence to 'correct' usage and to agree on what 'correct' usage should be. Their efforts were at various times promoted or jeopardised by political circumstances. On the whole they were favoured by social stability, political unification and strong government; but these favourable circumstances by no means always obtained. For example, in France during the sixteenth century grammarians were largely unsuccessful in imposing a linguistic norm, and historians of the French language agree on the reasons why. M.K.Pope writes of the sixteenth-century grammarians in France:

It is, however, in the main the political and social conditions of their age and the prematurity of their attempts that occasioned their failure. The fixing of linguistic usage, the codification of grammatical rule, is only possible when conditions of life are stable, when there is existent some recognized authority to make decisions, backed up by a sufficient weight of public opinion to enforce them. In the sixteenth century these conditions were almost entirely absent.[20]

Similarly, A. Ewert observes:

If their attempts at regularizing the spelling,... at settling doubtful points of pronunciation and formulating rules of syntax proved abortive, the explanation lies partly in the fact that, less fortunate than Malherbe and the grammarians of the seventeenth century, they could not rely upon the sanction of a fashionable 'bel usage' or the support of an official body such as the Academy. The lack of a spirit of discipline among writers and in society as a whole, the unequal level of culture even at the court, and finally the social and political upheaval of the Wars of Religion, rendered their efforts comparatively fruitless.[21]

In the following century, by contrast, conditions in France were much more favourable, and the alliance between grammarians and writers of national prestige prospered. Of this alliance there is no more conspicuous example on record than Racine submitting his verse to the grammarian Bouhours for criticism. That Shakespeare might have done anything comparable in the cultural climate of Elizabethan England is unthinkable. Dryden, on the other hand, did correct the syntax of his earlier works to eliminate instances infringing the grammarians' rule which condemns ending a sentence with a preposition (an example, as it happens, of a quite arbitrary proscription, based on a misguided comparison between English and Latin).

Linguists have sometimes supposed that there is a 'natural' basis for prescriptive grammar in the value judgments passed by speakers on one another's speech. Bloomfield, in the much cited paper on 'Literate and Illiterate Speech',[22] held that such value judgments reflect 'a generally human state of affairs, true in every group and applicable to all languages', where 'by a

[20] M.K.Pope, *From Latin to Modern French*, Manchester 1934, pp.44-5.
[21] A.Ewert, *The French Language*, London 1933, pp.12-13.
[22] *American Speech*, vol.2, 1927, pp.432-9.

cumulation of obvious superiorities, both of character and standing as well as language, some persons are felt to be better models of conduct and speech than others'. The evidence for this is dubious. The deliberate and regular inculcation of preferred forms of speech seems to arise usually in response to particular social conditions. Preservation of a culture in the face of threatened extinction or absorption is one such motivation. This may give rise even in illiterate communities to the public allocation of linguistic 'guardianship' to particular individuals, or the recognition of certain language-teaching duties as a social responsibility. (An instance of the former would be the institution of language 'monitors' among the Torres Strait Islanders.[23] An example of the latter would be the Blackfoot Indian custom of daily language lessons given by mothers to their male children during the winter months.[24]) But the systematisation of grammar involves more than this.

As P.Mühlhäusler points out in connexion with the Torres Strait case, the correction of speech involved differs significantly from European schoolmasters correcting their pupils' grammar. The corrections occur in a 'real' context, not in a teaching situation. There is no question of the grammaticality of decontextualised sentences. Mühlhäusler adds: 'Intuitions about that kind of grammaticality are notoriously unreliable or non-existent among speakers of many Pacific languages, in particular those with no training in a European standard language, as deciding on contextless grammaticality is not one of the metalinguistic games they tend to engage in.'[25]

In a cultural tradition where literacy was not at a premium, and where there were no social, political or economic pressures towards linguistic conformity, it is highly unlikely that anything like the Western concept of rules of grammar would have emerged. In this connexion it is interesting to note that in modern times Western observers have often commented on the apparent lack of concern with linguistic 'correctness' in pre-literate or semi-literate societies. In 1911 William Churchill wrote:

[23] L.G.Cromwell, 'Bar kar mir. To talk with no curves: important speaking among mainland Torres Strait Islanders', *Anthropological Forum*, vol.5 no.1, 1980-2.
[24] Chief Buffalo Child Long Lance, *Long Lance*, Alberta 1928, p.5.
[25] Mühlhäusler, op. cit.

> I do not know a single language of the Pacific in which it is
> possible to be ungrammatical; there is certainly not one in which
> certain persons are understood to speak with due regard for syntax
> and certain others betray their lack of education by speaking
> incorrectly. That is a distinction which marks only the races of
> higher culture...[26]

More recently W.J.Samarin reports that among the Gbeya of
Central Africa parents rarely if ever correct the speech of their
children, and the only concept they have of the difference
between good and bad speech is that bad speech is what causes
trouble between people.[27] In the same vein, Mühlhäusler
comments on the extreme linguistic tolerance of speakers of Tok
Pisin in Papua New Guinea:

> Whilst it is often assumed that one's own variey of Tok Pisin is the
> best or purest, other varieties are not looked down upon or called
> bad, unless they are bordering on the unintelligible.[28]

Such tolerance is plainly incompatible with the traditional
Western orthological view, the internal logic of which actually
requires linguistic deviance to be condemned. Otherwise, rules
would not be rules and grammarians would not be in business.

*   *   *

Given the deep entrenchment of orthological dogma in Western
attitudes towards language, at first it may seem unexpected to
find Saussure in the opening chapter of the *Cours de linguistique
générale* dismissing grammar as a primitive phase in the
development of linguistics because it aims 'solely at providing
rules which distinguish between correct and incorrect forms'.[29]
But he then goes on to acclaim grammatical analysis as
constituting the heart of synchronic linguistics, which disavows
any vested normative interests whatsoever. How can these two

---

[26] W.Churchill, *Beach-la-mar*, Washington 1911, p.15.
[27] W.J.Samarin, 'The art of Gbeya insults', *International Journal of American
Linguistics*, vol.35, 1969, pp.323-9.
[28] P.Mühlhäusler, 'Language and communicational efficiency: the case of Tok
Pisin', *Language & Communication*, vol.2 no.2, 1982, p.114.
[29] Saussure, op. cit., p.13.

positions be reconciled? How could grammar, for centuries nothing if not prescriptive, suddenly have become anything but prescriptive?

Part of the answer lies in the work of Saussure's immediate predecessors, the comparative philologists. In their eagerness to achieve scientific status for their linguistic studies by assimilating the discovery of linguistic patterns to the discovery of laws of Nature, they were more than content to sacrifice any distinction between rules and regularities. Dealing for the most part with languages long 'dead', they could afford to. They either failed to see the incoherence of supposing that rules of grammar are somehow inherent 'in the language', or else ignored it as an epistemological side-issue which could safely be left to philosophers to debate while linguists got on with the solid empirical work of excavating proto-Indo-European. Doubtless they would have been nonplussed by the criticism that what they were doing amounted to projecting modern prescriptivism back into linguistic pre-history, and belatedly setting themselves up as the grammarians their remote ancestors never had.

When Saussure dismisses grammatical prescriptivism he certainly does not mean to imply that it is a thing of the past. On the contrary, during his own lifetime it had grown in a quite dramatic way. In France especially, prescriptivism had taken on new and formidable aspects. The grammarian's linguistic legislation was now backed by state legislation. When, for example, the French Minister of Public Instruction in 1901, with the sanction of the Académie Française, decreed that the past participle followed by an infinitive may always be invariable, he laid down a rule of grammar which had to be taught to schoolchildren in every classroom in France. (Previously the rule had been that the past participle conjugated with *avoir* and followed by an infinitive agreed in gender and number with a preceding direct object, as in *les poissons que j'ai vus nager* 'the fish I saw swimming'.) Priscian and Donatus might well have envied the minister's authority to enact syntactic laws: they would certainly have been amazed by it. A state in which the government could do such things was surely a grammarians' paradise undreamt of in antiquity.

The advent of this grammarians' paradise was of relatively recent date. Universal literacy was not exactly an educational aim which had ever inspired Priscian and Donatus, any more than it had fired teachers of the *ars grammatica* in the medieval universities. That did not prevent the pedagogic wares of the traditional grammarian from being adapted and pressed into service for the programmes of popular education which were instituted in most countries of Western Europe during the course of the nineteenth century. 'Grammar for the people' might well have been the epigraph, for example, of William Cobbett's famous grammar of 1818, written expressly for 'the Soldier, the Sailor, the Apprentice, and the Ploughboy'; in short, for 'the Labouring Classes of the community'[30] in general. Cobbett's *Grammar* sold 10,000 copies in a month. During the next hundred years more manuals of elementary grammatical instruction were published than in the preceding two millennia. More people were being taught to speak and write *grammatically* (and not just to speak and write - the difference, as Cobbett makes clear, being what is important) during Saussure's lifetime than ever before. Grammar had become an essential article in the great charter of European educational reform. Since the proclaimed goal of educational reform was social improvement, and its immediate practical task the provision of literate and numerate employees for an expanding industrial and commercial society, grammar for the people from Cobbett onwards turned out to be predictably and profoundly prescriptivist. This is the background against which it should come as no surprise to find that the legacy of Priscian and Donatus is disputed in the courts of higher scholarship just when new elementary schools had claimed that legacy as public patrimony for general distribution.

Saussure was not in the least interested in advancing (or impeding) the cause of universal literacy: his primary concern was with the academic autonomy of his subject. But he was obliged to take into account, as any intelligent theorist in his place would have done, that the successful nationalisation of grammar in the interests of state education was already a *fait accompli*. This forced him to seek a compromise which would restore grammar to the province of science and intellectual respectability, while leaving the syntax of the past participle to its fate at the hands of the Ministry of Public Instruction. It was a necessary compromise, because Saussurean synchronicity

---

[30] W.Cobbett, *A Grammar of the English Language*, London 1818, p.iii.

needed grammar. The result of that compromise was the Saussurean theory of the language machine.

Saussure was nothing if not an astute academic strategist. Having adroitly fended off the competing claims of experimental psychology and neurophysiology, he had no intention of surrendering language tamely to the teaching profession. At the same time, he clearly could not afford to cut linguistics off from its pedagogic roots in the Western tradition altogether. For he was in no position to offer a wholesale replacement for the long established terminological apparatus of traditional grammar. What he needed, therefore, was an independent basis on which to redefine the function of the grammarian in strictly non-normative terms, while retaining as much of the old-fashioned pedagogic terminology as might come in useful. Positing a language machine in the brain was the ideal solution. The individual's internal systematisation of *la langue* then becomes purely mechanical, and the grammarian can study it but cannot interfere with it. Moreover, being purely mechanical, the systematisation requires no external motivation at all. Grammatical rules at a stroke become internal cognitive rules, devoid of prescriptive implications or social consequences. Thus, while proclaiming *la langue* to be a social reality, Saussurean linguistics attributes the constitution of this reality in the individual to automatic machinery over which no one, literate or illiterate, grammarian or ignoramus, has any control.

How seriously Saussure intended an investigation of the cerebral mechanics of grammar to be pursued is another matter. Almost certainly not as seriously as it was by a later generation of scholars in the cognitive sciences. Their endorsement of his strategic manoeuvre he could hardly have objected to, although their literal-minded acceptance of internalised grammatical rules he would probably have regarded as extremely naive. One must stress in this connexion that Saussure's linguistic thinking was entirely uninfluenced by any of the developments which were later to acquire such prestige in linguistic circles. He did not live to witness the rise of behaviourism or wonder at the modern empire of mathematical logic. He had never seen a sound spectrogram, let alone a computer print-out. The phrase *artificial intelligence* would probably have struck him as a contradiction in terms. Nevertheless, it remains true that where language is concerned it was Saussure who brought the equation 'man = machine' seriously into the twentieth century's theoretical reckoning.

It would be a mistake to put this down to intellectual eccentricity on the part of Saussure, or to see him as exemplifying the 'genius-in-advance-of-his-time' stereotype either. On the contrary, he was very much of his time, and so was his linguistic thinking. Despite his protests about grammar and his shrewd academic tactics, it is remarkable how uncritically Saussure accepted the basic sociolinguistic assumptions of the period in European history in which he lived and of the social class to which he belonged. This tacit acceptance is evident not only from the theoretical idealisations which Saussure proposes or presupposes, but also from the linguistic issues which are never raised in the *Cours* at all.

For instance, Saussure evidently saw the linguistically 'normal' individual as being a monoglot, and the linguistically 'normal' community as being a monoglot community. Bilingualism or multilingualism are apparently 'unnatural' conditions for Saussure, and he never discusses them. Since Saussure himself was Swiss and his family had been established in Switzerland for generations, this is at first sight quite astonishing. It throws into even sharper relief the extent to which Saussure's thinking was influenced by the dominant trend in Europe towards the sociopolitical ideal of 'one nation: one language'. It is this sociopolitical ideal which Saussurean linguistics accepts without argument and generalises for all linguistic communities.

Again, the *Cours* devotes several chapters to geographical variation in language, but none to social stratification. A Martian reading Saussure would get the impression that in every linguistic community on Earth the highest and the lowest members spoke exactly alike, and that there were no linguistic divisions reflecting differences of income, occupation or social status. There never seem to be any foreigners or ethnic minorities in the Saussurean linguistic community either. Or perhaps the Martian would have to assume that *in spite of* sociolinguistic advantages and disadvantages, all citizens in maturity ended up linguistically equal, presumably having been brought up to speak alike, and having equal access to all educational facilities. Whatever the explanation, in the Saussurean linguistic community such divisions have been theoretically 'normalised' out of existence.

As regards geographical variation, what emerges as Saussure's view is that the linguistic map is ideally (he says 'naturally') one without boundaries of any kind. However, historical events of one sort or another have upset this ideal state of affairs, so that the map we have is rather sharply partitioned into discrete homogeneous areas. (Where those areas correspond to political boundaries, patently, the ideal 'one nation: one language' is already realised.) Within the major homogeneous areas, differences between one locality and the next tend to dissolve into an evenly spread gradation of very minor divergences in pronunciation, morphology and vocabulary. These divergences are always too slight to provide any serious obstacle to communication, apparently, or to act as irritants for political tensions or social grievances within the community. The individual points in geographical space seem to correspond to small, idealised villages, where the speech may differ very slightly from that of the next village up the road, but itself is internally uniform. Thus in Saussurean linguistic cartography it is as if language had been painted on the face of the earth in the even, well-delineated colours of a school atlas. The political map and the linguistic map are not exactly identical, but correspond to a rough approximation. France is green, Germany brown and Britain red, while in the English Channel there is no language: blue stands for water.

One of the ironies in all this which Saussure almost certainly failed to appreciate was that the grammatical prescriptivism he went out of his way to condemn as offering 'no scientific or objective approach'[31] to linguistic phenomena was in all probability the major obstacle he never overcame in his own thinking. That prescriptivism was in any case responsible in large measure for bringing about a sociolinguistic situation in the context of which Saussure's linguistic theories look *prima facie* more plausible than they otherwise might. This was because prescriptivist programmes of grammar for the people were in fact successful. By the time Saussure died they had contributed to linguistic standardisation on a scale Europe had not seen since the days of the Roman empire. Local dialects were everywhere in decline, their eventual demise hastened by educational syllabuses based on the national language. Regional literary traditions were dead or dying, those who strove to maintain them

---

[31] Saussure, loc. cit.

increasingly stigmatised as quaint rustics, out of touch with the modern world. Europe's apparently relentless progress towards national linguistic uniformity itself reinforced prescriptivism, which in turn accelerated that progress. Language in the grammarians' paradise of the late nineteenth century was locked into a prescriptivist circle.

Saussurean linguistics reflects that circularity (and even allegorises it in the form of a *circuit de la parole*) but entirely fails to diagnose its causes. Politicians and educationalists were on this level far more clearsighted than linguistic theorists. The Disraeli who introduced the famous Act of 1876 which heralded a society which (unlike Rousseau's) would *compel* every child to learn to read and write a prescribed language was the same Disraeli who, thirty years earlier, had described the conditions of British mineworkers in his novel *Sybil* and asked:

> Can we wonder at the hideous coarseness of their language, when we remember the savage rudeness of their lives?[32]

But it had taken British politicians those thirty years to realise that grammar for the people and the associated idea of 'the career open to talent' was not, as the *Encyclopaedia Britannica*[33] authoritatively informed its readers in 1910, 'a matter of abstract humanitarian theory' but 'a cogent practical necessity imposed by the fierce international competition which prevails in the arts and industries of life'. For any 'nation that is not to fail in the struggle for commercial success' what Disraeli's Act provided was not a domestic social luxury but an international survival kit in a Darwinian economic world.

This was the world into which Saussure was born in 1857.[34] His family circumstances and his residence in a succession of academic ivory towers in Paris and Geneva may have made it difficult for him to come to grips with certain aspects of that world. According to all the biographical evidence, his eyes were firmly fixed in his student days on linguistic horizons dimly discernible in the mists of Indo-European prehistory. Nothing in

[32] *Sybil*, London 1845, p.161.
[33] 'Education', 11th ed., vol.8, p.960.
[34] Not 1871, as the latest (1986) reprint of the only (semi-official) biography still insists: 'Notes biographiques et critiques sur F.de Saussure', *Cours de linguistique générale*, ed. T.de Mauro, Paris, p.319.

what he subsequently wrote suggests that his intellectual gaze ever altered. What Saussure personally sought seems to have been a theoretical justification for that fixed focus. One of the attractions of Saussurean linguistics is the facility with which it seems able to bring into focus no less easily a linguistic past than a linguistic present. Sanskrit becomes as accessible as Spanish, dead languages (provided their written texts survive) as amenable to Saussurean analysis as living ones. But that impressive levelling of past and present is purchased by not asking certain questions, thereby disconnecting the linguistic system from the social system altogether.

* * *

Language functioning in its social context, on the contrary, was the overriding public concern of the politicians and educationalists who were Saussure's contemporaries. The combination of national commercial self-interest with moral uplift was a form of motivation which in the nineteenth century rarely failed to elicit public action. It was a motivation quite overtly appealed to in Britain, and one cannot suppose its appeal was lost on Britain's economic competitors, even though they might have found it less than decorous to proclaim it openly *à l'anglaise*. (From Waterloo onwards, the British were condemned to be the cultural louts of Europe.) The case for prescriptivism thus became indistinguishable from the case for standardisation. This is clearly reflected in the linguistic history of the term *standard* itself in its application to the national languages of Europe (*standard English, standard French*, etc.), a usage which does not become common until the mid-century. That it is an English usage in origin is all the more remarkable in view of the fact that, unlike France, England had never established an Academy to act as an official watchdog body and determine what was good English and what was not. Furthermore, early Victorian England was anything but the homogeneous linguistic community of the kind later idealised in Saussurean theory. To conjure up a 'standard English' as the 'national language' of English-speaking people was to invent a sociolinguistic fiction.

Nevertheless, the contention that a standard language had long existed in England (even if no one had been quite sure what it was) came to play an important role in the 1850s in connexion with the major lexicographical project which eventually resulted in the publication of the *Oxford English Dictionary*, under the editorship of James Murray. Before that project was launched, most English people had almost certainly never heard of 'standard English'. The earliest attestation of the expression given by the *O.E.D. Supplement* of 1933 is dated 1858, and it comes from the text of the original proposals for the dictionary itself. (There can hardly be a more blatant example in intellectual history of attempting retrospective validation by means of self-quotation.)

Murray's approach to lexicography typifies the prescriptivism which Saussure regarded as characteristic of the traditional grammarian. Murray himself made no claims to be either a grammarian or linguistic theorist, but his influence on linguistic theory may in the end have been no less profound than Saussure's. He was born twenty years before Saussure and outlived him by two. Unlike Saussure, he did not come from an academically privileged background, and never attended a university. He began his career as a more or less self-taught schoolmaster from the Borders, who clearly regarded himself as a mere outsider seeking admittance to the inner sanctum of English language and culture. He was a firm believer in authority in the matter of laying down rights and wrongs of English usage. As he admitted later to Henry Sweet, he had been obliged to learn a different pronunciation of English from that which he personally had been brought up to use, in order to teach English 'correctly' to his pupils. Indeed, he cited this fact as a qualification when Sweet questioned his competence in English phonetics.[35] Murray projected this personal pedagogic view of correct usage on to the whole enterprise of tracing the history of English vocabulary.

There is no doubt that the *Oxford English Dictionary* as a major lexicographical project, of national importance, dedicated to and approved by Queen Victoria herself, had a vested interest in the thesis that there was a variety of English which was its 'standard' form. That was central to the rationale of its plan, and to its inclusion and exclusion of words and meanings. Murray was already claiming the existence of standard English as a

---

[35] K.M.E.Murray, *Caught in the Web of Words*, New Haven/London 1977, p.190.

historical fact in the 1870s. For some time, however, the term *standard English* found itself in competition with various alternatives, including *received English* and *Classical English*. These expressions became prominent in the course of a prolonged nineteenth-century discussion of growing momentum, which was to have profound implications for the establishment of a national school system in Britain, and to result eventually in the displacement of the Classics in favour of the study of English as the linguistic basis of education.

The most revealing nineteenth-century rival to the term *standard English* is undoubtedly *Classical English*. It is no accident that this expression is modelled on *Classical Latin*. Educational reform in Victorian England was in need of an alternative to the existing 'public school' syllabus, already available to the children of families affluent enough to afford it. For public school education was based on the Classical languages, and these were thought to be too difficult for children of the British working classes to have any hope of learning. It was to fill this gap that the myth of 'standard English' was invented, although the term *Classical English* perhaps points more clearly to what was regarded as being needed (an indigenous educational equivalent of Classical Latin). Part and parcel of the myth, from its inception, was the patronising assumption that although the children of the working classes could speak some kind of English without the benefit of going to school, it was only a very inferior kind of English. It needed to be 'improved' if the speaker were to become, as Cobbett's *English Grammar* puts it, 'an object of respect'.

Promotion of the idea of standard English in that context was firmly associated with the equation: 'standard' = 'best'. This value judgment is actually incorporated into the 1933 *O.E.D. Supplement* definition of the word *standard*, which describes it as 'applied to the variety of the speech of a country which, by reason of its cultural status and currency, is held to represent the best form of that speech'. This reflects a widely held Victorian belief in the virtues of competition. The evolution of modern English was seen as the outcome of a kind of collective national competition for the 'best' usage, just as the languages of the world were seen as being in competition to be selected as best suited for international needs. In 1862 one appeal for volunteer helpers in the national dictionary project refers explicitly to 'the race of English words which is to form the dominant speech of the world'.[36] The connexion between the myth of standard English and Victorian imperialism could scarcely be plainer. If English was to achieve world dominance, it must offer a standard or model for non-native-speakers to adopt, and that model must be 'the best'. (It is worth recalling in this connexion that the practical demand for such a programme was already making itself felt overseas, following the decision taken in 1835 to insist on English as the medium of education throughout India. That decision had been taken mainly on the advocacy of T.B.Macaulay, President of the Committee of Public Instruction, whose incomprehension of and contempt for traditional Hindu scholarship were alike profound.)

The prize in the international competition, then, was recognition as 'world language'. The corresponding prize in the national competition was deemed to be recognition by a cultural élite, and hence adoption as their literary language. Historically, the competition had allegedly begun in the fifteenth century, when for the first time the question 'Which is the best variety of English?' began to be taken seriously. The *locus classicus* endlessly cited in support of this rather simple-minded account of the history of English is Caxton's well-known complaint about the lack of uniformity in English usage and the difficulty of knowing which kind of English a writer ought to adopt.

Murray's commitment to the 'cultural competition' theory of the evolution of English is most evident in his *Encyclopaedia Britannica* articles. In one interesting instance, his revision for the 11th edition actually substitutes the phrase 'Standard English' (in quotes) for what in the 9th edition he had called ' "English" *par excellence*'. Adopting the competition theory allowed Murray to ignore the fact that the usage of the cultural élite in the nineteenth century simply did not function as an 'English *par excellence*' for the majority of his fellow countrymen, because they neither spoke nor wrote it. Doubtless he viewed this as a merely temporary deficiency soon to be remedied by the programme of state education which had begun rather hesitantly in 1832, but by 1876 had got as far as Disraeli's Act which for the first time proclaimed: 'it shall be the duty of the parent of every child to cause such child to receive efficient

[36] Murray, op. cit., p.137.

elementary instruction in reading, writing and arithmetic'. Given sufficient optimism, it was perhaps understandable that the equation of standard English with national norm, and that in turn with dominant international language, should be treated as a foregone historical conclusion. The Victorians were never very good at distinguishing between facts, ideals and good intentions.

Although the *O.E.D.* purported to be a dictionary 'on historical principles', the historical principles invoked are covertly teleological. That teleology is part of the myth which represented the obscure processes of linguistic evolution as conspiring to evolve the 'best' variety of nineteenth-century English. Thus the dubious Victorian marriage of historical lexicography with educational reform produced the even more dubious offspring of a 'standard language' credited with that mysterious diachronic identity through change, indiscernible to any eye but the less-than-impartial philologist's. Intrinsic to the reformers' programme, inevitably, was the notion that there existed a national consensus as to which the best variety of English actually was. Nor is it surprising that the variety thus selected should be the variety identified by those who considered themselves 'educated' as their own: which happened to be, for obvious reasons, a kind of English spoken by a somewhat narrow social stratum of that period, certainly not one to which Murray's family belonged. Murray was an example of a man from a fairly humble background who had had to work hard in order to 'better himself'. For him, the 'best' English was the English identified with that bettered state, as it was to be for many. But that was not the sense of 'best' which the nineteenth-century 'cultural competition' theory of English officially admitted to.

Once the decision had been taken by the Victorian reformers to uphold one particular variety of modern English as 'the best', it became important to set a historical seal of approval upon that choice. This is where the publication of the *O.E.D.* played such an important role. Regardless of the fact that the linguistic usage currently designated 'the best' might actually conflict in various ways with the linguistic usage of former times, it was necessary to show the currently proclaimed 'best English' as having impeccable ancestry, descended directly from the users of the 'best English' of earlier ages. It was here that the term *standard* proved ideal: for it had long been used of literary works and authors acknowledged to be both authoritative and exemplary.

The word *standard* proved ideally suited to the purpose of the Victorian reformers for another reason too: it conveniently suggested in advance a uniformity and general acceptance which disguised the fact that the particular form of English being idealised was a form which only a small minority of the English-language community ever used. Calling this form 'standard English' implied an accessibility to all, flagrantly contradicted by the social and linguistic situation actually obtaining in Victorian England. It is significant that the first recorded use of the expression in 1844 shows it occurring in the phrase 'our standard English'.[37] The *our* already had overtones of national unity and common cultural heritage.

The expression *standard English* was also ideal for a third reason. It is no coincidence that the term found favour at the same time as the emergent Victorian belief in the millennium of commercial prosperity based on the rationalisation of methods of manufacture made available by the Industrial Revolution. The key to this prosperity was indeed standardisation. Eli Whitney, now generally acknowledged as the first industrialist to realise the potential of standardised components in mass production, put the idea to the test in his government contracts for arms manufacture in the early 1800s. It was his success which give the word *standard* its modern industrial and commercial connotation; and it can hardly be accidental that those who began to use the term *standard English* in Victorian England belonged to the first generation who had the opportunity of assimilating the lessons of Whitney's achievement and what it meant for the future of modern industrialised society. The first attestation of the term antedates by just seven years that monument to Victorian commercial enterprise, the Great Exhibition of 1851.

The idea that a nation could profit from standardising society through universal education went hand in hand with the notion that industry can profit from standardising manufacturing processes. Many people of Murray's generation identified both ideas with progress. Intrinsic to that notion of progress, needless to say, was the belief that the national interest was to be identified with promoting assumptions, ideals, norms of

---

[37] E.Guest, 'On English pronouns personal', *Proceedings of the Philological Society*, vol.1. This example antedates the earliest cited in the O.E.D. For the reference I am indebted to Mr. A.E.Crowley.

behaviour and even forms of speech which were in fact those of a certain English social class; just as it was assumed that the well-being of the international community of peoples was best served by securing British Imperial dominance in world affairs.

Henry Sweet stood the truth of the matter on its head when he wrote in 1908 that 'Standard English... is now a class-dialect more than a local dialect': for this implies that it was not always so. In other words, Sweet tacitly accepts the mythical projection back into history of a concept which had reached maturity only in his own lifetime. Standard English had not 'become' a class-dialect: it was a class-dialect which had 'become' something neologistically called 'standard English'.

According to Sweet,[38] standard English was already in 1908 'the language of the educated all over Great Britain', an identification which fudges precisely the issue of who exactly the educated are, and what counts as education. Daniel Jones was more forthright about this matter of education when he described Received Pronunciation as 'that generally used by those who have been educated at preparatory boarding schools and the "Public Schools" '. To put the matter beyond doubt he adds the footnote: ' "Public School" in the English sense, not in the American sense.'[39] In adopting the term *Received Pronunciation* in preference to *Standard Pronunciation*, Jones explicitly disavowed the more questionable assumptions associated with the term *standard*. 'I do not consider it possible at the present time', he wrote, 'to regard any special type as "Standard" or as intrinsically "better" than other types.'[40] Clearly not everyone had been taken in by Murray's Victorian myth of standard English. In 1914 Shaw satirised the whole idea with memorable wit in his play *Pygmalion*, which caricatures Sweet as the Professor Higgins who undertakes the linguistic transformation of a guttersnipe flower girl into a duchess. (The flower girl's name was Eliza. It was also the name subsequently chosen by Weizenbaum[41] for his famous linguistic computer program, perhaps the first actually to have deceived the

[38] Cited in the *O.E.D.*, 1933 Supplement, art. *standard*.
[39] D.Jones, *An Outline of English Phonetics*, 9th ed., Cambridge 1964, p.12. (First published 1918.)
[40] ibid.
[41] J.Weizenbaum, 'ELIZA - A Computer Program for the Study of Natural Language Communication between Man and Machine', *Communications of the Association for Computing Machinery* vol.9, 1966.

unsuspecting into believing they were communicating with a human being and not a machine. Higgins' Eliza, unlike Weizenbaum's, eventually rebelled against her programmer.)

The irony of Jones' denial that there was any standard form of English pronunciation was that in spite of his protests, his own careful description of the socially restricted variety which he called 'Received Pronunciation' was immediately taken as the model for 'standard English'. His *English Pronouncing Dictionary* went through no less than seventeen reprintings and revised editions between 1917 and 1945. In this respect, he did for pronunciation what Murray had done for vocabulary: established an explicit 'black-and-white' codification which could be treated as authoritative for prescriptive purposes. His unavailing disclaimers are themselves the clearest indication of how irresistible the prescriptivist pressures had become to transform the myth of a national language into a social reality.

* * *

The case history of 'standard English' provides an instructive example of the orthological miracles possible in a grammarians' paradise. Saussurean linguistics provides a no less instructive example of how it is possible in paradise for miracles to pass unnoticed.

As contemporaries, Murray and Saussure make an interesting pair. Murray, earnestly ensnared in his own 'web of words', was oblivious to the theoretical implications of his work but not to its national importance, for which he duly received a knighthood. Saussure, preoccupied with theorising about an internal language machine, ignored a much more powerful language machine outside: the language machine of standardisation, now driven by systems of compulsory education.

Saussure in the end failed to see that the 'work' plausibly attributable to any internal linguistic machinery will depend on the 'work' already done by external machinery in society. The linguistic equation 'man = machine' only begins to seem credible in the context of a system of social control capable of maintaining a high degree of linguistic conformity. Non-conformity is never conducive to mechanical explanations. Curiously blind to the forces shaping the linguistic communities of Europe during his own lifetime, Saussure was the last person likely to grasp the profound social significance of the new type of linguistic theory he was instrumental in introducing.

Chapter Six

Paradise Lost

Neville Cardus in his *Autobiography* recounts an incident which occurred in about 1920 when the redoubtable C.P.Scott was editor of the *Manchester Guardian* and Cardus a junior member of its staff.

> In my hurry one night to send up the Miscellany column to the composing-room, I allowed a contributed paragraph to get into print with 'from thence' in it. As soon as I saw the paper next morning I knew I was, as they say, 'for it.' Scott went through every column lynx-eyed, all excepting the market reports. Sure as death, he tackled me without delay. His whiskers clove the air when I entered his room. 'You should know by now', he said with infinite charm and menace, 'that the term "from thence" is not English and is therefore banned from the *Manchester Guardian*. A man might as well say "to thither." '
>
> With the bravery of the young I retaliated. I knew as well as Scott himself that 'from thence' is vile, but some devil took hold of me, and I pointed out to him that there were precedents for the use of 'from thence' in the works of accredited masters of English literature.
>
> 'Really?' he queried, aiming an arrow at me from his eye, 'and pray where?'
>
> 'In Henry Fielding in general, and *Tom Jones* in particular,' I brazenly replied.
>
> Without hesitation he said, with a delicacy of accent that froze my marrow, 'Really? Well, my dear fellow, all I can say is that Mr. Fielding would not use "from thence" twice on my newspaper. Good-night.'[1]

A linguistics of cognitive machinery, as introduced by Saussure and developed by his successors, can say nothing that is worth saying about the language of such an episode as this; even

---

[1] N.Cardus, *Autobiography*, London 1947, pp.112-13.

though – or perhaps, one is tempted to say, precisely because – language is at the very centre of the episode in question. Least of all can any grammar of cognitive rules tell us anything about the grammaticality of *from thence*, even though grammaticality is claimed to be at the heart of the cognitive grammarian's concerns. (All we shall be told if we press the inquiry is that *from thence* is grammatical in those varieties of English whose rules it does not infringe, and ungrammatical in all others. Perhaps for good measure we might be given a mathematical symbolisation of the rules themselves, as if this were an explanation. But that the grammaticality of *from thence* is in dispute we already understood if we understood Cardus' story at all; and if we did not know it before, we could certainly have gathered it from the story as told. A so-called grammarian who can say no more about the rights and wrongs of the matter than that would have been drummed out of the profession in Quintilian's day. But nowadays saying anything more about *from thence* will be condemned as prescriptivism.)

What Cardus is describing in admirably plain English cannot be captured in any systems of rule-formulae: it is the working of the linguistic machinery in the world 'outside', which Saussure ignored. The machinery in question here is none other than that of the 'standard English' machine set up by the Victorian educational reforms. (The full piquancy of the anecdote is lost unless the reader knows that by 1920 young Cardus counted only as minimally 'educated', having left school in the Manchester slums at thirteen. Hence the audacity of his grammatical pitched battle with Scott, and the effrontery of citing literary sources as evidence.) That Cardus learnt more about language by working on the *Manchester Guardian* under Scott than he would have done by studying Saussure or other linguistic theorists is not the point. (*Mutatis mutandis*, the same would undoubtedly be true today.) The point is that what Cardus tells us reveals a dimension of prescriptivism which both the theorists of cognitive machinery and the champions of 'standard English' pass over in silence. What is ultimately at stake for Cardus is his job.

The fundamental distinction between 'descriptive grammar' and 'prescriptive grammar', on which modern linguistic theory simultaneously bases its commitment to the former and its disdain of the latter, has always depended for any superficial credibility it might have either on a serious underestimation of the difference in linguistic mentality between literate and pre-literate societies, or else on a naive misconception of what prescriptivism entails. Or on both. The misconception is epitomised in Saussure's dismissal of prescriptive grammar *in toto* with the simplistic explanation that its aim is 'providing rules which distinguish between correct and incorrect forms'.[2] In this misconception he was followed uncritically and is followed still by many academic linguists wishing to distance their profession from that of schoolteaching. (They may deny in public that any professional snobbery is involved, but the denial rings hollow.) The misconception is twofold. In the first place it confuses a particular form of grammatical prescriptivism with its linguistic functions. (To provide rules is no more the 'aim' of grammar – and never had been – than providing logarithms is the 'aim' of mathematics.) In the second place it obscures the fact that the functions of grammatical prescriptivism vary widely, and vary according to the sociolinguistic context. Consequently, any global condemnation in the name of linguistic theory merely substitutes stereotyping for critical analysis.

More worrying than this is that, having failed to see Saussure's mistake in the first place, his successors should actually set themselves up as experts with a 'scientific' obligation to combat the alleged linguistic errors of the benighted grammarian. One wonders what Cardus and C.P.Scott would have made of the solemn moralising of the following passage:

> Linguists see it as their duty to correct the bias of traditional grammar and traditional language-teaching. Until recently, grammarians have been concerned almost exclusively with the language of literature and have taken little account of everyday colloquial speech. All too often they have treated the norms of literary usage as the norms of correctness for the language itself and have condemned colloquial usage, in so far as it differs from literary usage, as ungrammatical, slovenly or even illogical.[3]

If only those duty-conscious linguists had been able to spread the true grammatical gospel in the dark North of the 1920s, perhaps life on the staff of the *Manchester Guardian* would have been a

[2] Saussure, op. cit., p.13.
[3] J.Lyons, *Language and Linguistics*, Cambridge 1981, p.11.

kinder and a happier one.

> 'Splendid, Cardus! I see you've split another infinitive on the Sports Page. Now that's *real* English! Take a rise of a penny a week.'

Cardus and Scott might also have been pardonably perplexed by some of the reasons linguists have given for condemning the grammarian's criteria of correctness: for example,

> Normative grammar teaches us to say *It is I* instead of *It's me*, to avoid sentences ending with prepositions, to know the difference between *owing to* and *due to*, to use *each other* instead of *one another* when only two people are involved, and so on. The authority of those 'correct' forms lies, of course, in the grammar books ... Most of these rules of grammar have no real justification and there is therefore no serious reason for condemning the 'errors' they proscribe. What is correct and what is not correct is only a matter of what is accepted by society. If everyone says *It's me*, then surely *It's me* is correct English.[4]

The lynx-eyed Scott would certainly not have failed to spot the *non sequitur* in the last sentence, while Cardus might well have pointed out that Quintilian used much the same arguments as these, but in *defence* of normative grammar.

It is a travesty of the history of grammar to represent prescriptivism as relying invariably or typically on dubious criteria. It is no less a travesty of reasoning to argue against it that there is only one correct interpretation of correctness (that being, needless to say, the linguist's). All this does is replace one form of prescriptivism by another. The thesis that if everyone says *x* then *x* is correct requires rather more support than vague appeal to a conventionalist theory of language: for, as the Greeks and Romans knew, a conventionalist theory of language is entirely compatible with normative grammar. Uniformity of practice does not license the inference that any uniform practice is right, and the social world would be a very odd place if it did. The linguistic theorist who maintains the extreme view that saying *x* is correct if everyone says it is like the legal theorist who holds that the law is simply what everyone does. In short, what lies behind this variety of anti-prescriptivism is the well-known

[4] F.R.Palmer, *Grammar*, 2nd ed., Harmondsworth 1984, pp.15-16.

positivist reduction of rules to regularities, and a concomitant failure to grasp the concept of normative activity altogether.

In its most polemic form, this issues in categoric denials that language has any element of normativity whatsoever: for instance,

> There is no such thing as good and bad (or correct and incorrect, grammatical and ungrammatical, right and wrong) in language.[5]

Here we see the self-righteous linguist attempting to throw the luckless prescriptive grammarian out of paradise altogether. What is revealing is the determination to carry out the expulsion even at the Pyrrhic cost of effacing any remaining distinction between linguistic theory and lunacy.

If modern linguistics is committed to preaching anti-prescriptivism as a 'duty', all one can say is that its own pedagogic practice belies what it preaches. Anyone who supposes that somehow linguists have managed to purge the notion of a grammatical rule from all normative implications would do well to look at the 'students' exercises' commonly given in university textbooks of general linguistics. Here we find all the normative horrors of preferring *It is I* to *It's me* jacked up one level further in the intellectual hierarchy. Lists of 'correct' sentences are provided, with instructions such as 'Write a grammar to generate these sentences, using phrase-structure rules and a lexicon', and admonitions like 'Be sure that your grammar doesn't generate any ungrammatical strings'.[6] Quintilian's *grammaticus* would surely have been delighted by this classic conflation between what the teacher tells the student to do in order to get full marks and what the rules tell the rule-follower to do in order to produce grammatical sentences. Doubtless students incapable of distinguishing the two will qualify for a degree in linguistics in no time at all.

Such examples highlight another aspect of the anti-prescriptivist witch-hunt in modern linguistics. The normative grammarian is no sooner evicted from paradise than his intellectual stock-in-trade is confiscated by his evictors. The very rules he was condemned for peddling turn up on the linguist's stall, sometimes – but not always – with new labels on

[5] R.A.Hall, *Leave Your Language Alone*, Ithaca 1950, p.6.
[6] Fromkin and Rodman, op. cit., p.239.

them. How is the claim that the rules have now been purged of prescriptive implications justified? Is it, indeed, a coherent claim at all?

One way of making it appear that the rules on offer now have a quite different status is to refer to them as if they were inherent 'in the language': or even as if the rules constituted the language itself. A typical example of this way of talking is:

> Nothing compels me to learn Russian, but if I choose to, I must abide by the rules of Russian phonology, syntax and semantics. For the Russian language *is* essentially the interlocking system of those rules.[7]

Although there is no mention of a 'language machine' here, the notion is clearly latent. Russian is being likened to an apparatus, which you can choose to use, or not. However, if you choose to use it, then as with any other machine, you would be abusing it or wrecking it if you perversely tried to do anything other than what the machine is designed for. It is rather like being told:

> Nothing obliges you to ride a bicycle; but if you choose to then you must be willing to coordinate your physical efforts in ways determined in advance by the relative positions of the wheels, saddle, handlebars, etc. and their interconnexions. For the bicycle just *is* the structure constituted by those parts and their interconnexions.

This kind of story certainly makes sense in the case of describing what a bicycle is and what is involved in learning to ride one. But does it make sense in the case of Russian?

No one tells us that the rules for riding a bicycle *constitute* the machine (which would be gibberish). But that seems to be just what is being claimed for the language: its rules have somehow 'become' its constituent parts.

There is a conceptual muddle here about language which is roughly on a par with supposing that if we formulate rules of harmony correctly then we are in some way describing the structure of a musical instrument, or of instruments of a certain class. What would be wrong with this is the same as what is wrong in the linguistic case. Rules of harmony no more inhere in a piano or in a violin than rules of grammar inhere in a language,

[7] M.Black, *The Labyrinth of Language*, Harmondsworth 1968, p.77.

and describing the (musical) structure of a piano or violin, if that is what we wish to do, is quite a different enterprise from setting down rules of harmony to be followed in playing or composing for it.

How does the muddle arise in the linguistic case? It arises from trying to find a plausible function for non-prescriptive rule-formulations. Somehow, it is supposed, these formulations must *describe* something. It is part of the puzzle which arises from confiscating the evicted grammarian's pedagogic terminology lock, stock and barrel. What is to be made, for instance, of 'the adjective agrees with its noun in gender, number and case' once it is stipulated that this formulation is *not* to be construed as expressing a prescriptive rule? It seems that if any validity is to be ascribed to it at all (and here the linguist finds it difficult to shake off the effects of a prescriptive education, because it goes against the grain to say the traditional rule-formulation is just 'wrong' or 'meaningless') the validity must be a descriptive validity. So a fact or object of some kind has to be found for the hallowed formulation to stand for. It is at this point that the linguist falls unwitting victim to the surrogationalism[8] which is endemic in Western linguistic thinking. Rules, as constitutive items of linguistic structure, are simply surrogationalist projections from 'de-prescriptivised' rule-formulations. There is no more telling example of what modern linguistics owes to its pervasive (but unacknowledged) commitment to surrogationalism. Far from having the (largely illusory) objectivity of the natural sciences (which it likes to claim), modern linguistics constantly projects into its analysis of language the biasses and assumptions of a particular cultural tradition, even while overtly disavowing them.

The result is that formulations like 'the adjective agrees with its noun in gender, number and case' become Janus-faced. Originally prescriptive, they are now provided with conjured-up 'structural facts' to which they can stand as 'descriptions'. The attraction of this for the linguistic theorist is that it simultaneously makes available a justification for the duplicity involved in peddling the grammarian's confiscated wares. It can now be claimed that where the prescriptive grammarian's rules were 'good' rules, that was because they really (unbeknown to

[8] R.Harris, *The Language-Makers*, London 1980, Ch.2.

their benighted formulators) corresponded to genuine structural features 'in' the language. But of course those lucky coincidences do not redeem prescriptive rules 'as such'. In other words, the gates of paradise remain firmly locked. No readmission for the normative charlatans.

The obvious alternative to finding a home for the new non-prescriptive rules by locating them 'in the language' itself is to find a home for them inside the language-user. This alternative is usually couched in carefully worded generalisations such as:

> every speaker of a language has mastered and internalized a generative grammar that expresses his knowledge of his language.[9]

It is to be noted that whereas the old pedagogic rules were said to be 'learnt' (or even, in the worst cases, 'beaten' into the hapless pupil), nothing so crude happens with these new linguistic rules: instead, they are 'mastered'. When it comes to explaining how this is done, the familiar rumble of cognitive machinery is heard. According to proponents of the new doctrine, 'mastering' the rules is a matter of 'internalising' them. The word *internalise* seems to suggest that the rules were not internal to start with, but in some way end up 'inside' the person who has 'mastered' them. Where 'inside'? In the brain, we are told, where they are 'represented'. What form do these cerebral 'representations' take? That, it seems, unfortunately no one knows. Perhaps one day neurophysiologists will find out for us.

Any simpleton who asks at this point how we can be sure about these rules in the brain if no one knows how they are 'represented' will be told that it stands to reason that the brain must have such 'representations' because otherwise no one could possibly have 'internalised' the rules, and unless the rules were 'internalised' a person could not have 'mastered' them, and therefore by definition would not know the language. But clearly we *do* know languages. With this compellingly circular demonstration the simpleton is expected to rest content.

More persistent sceptics who query the 'mechanical mythology of rules',[10] pointing out that cerebral 'representations' *prima*

---

[9] A.N.Chomsky, *Aspects of the Theory of Syntax*, Cambridge, Mass. 1965, p.8.
[10] G.P.Baker and P.M.S.Hacker, *Language, Sense and Nonsense*, Oxford 1984, pp.294ff.

facie require cerebral signs or symbols in which to be 'represented', will be fobbed off in one of two ways. One way is to concede that indeed it would be impossible to master a language unless one already had a prior language in the brain in which to 'represent' the rules of the language being mastered, and we are therefore forced to conclude that our brain does have such a language, which is 'the language of thought'.[11] The other way of dealing with 'representational scepticism' is just the opposite. This is to concede that there is an unsolved problem about *what* exactly 'representations' are in neurophysiological terms, but it doesn't matter because everybody else is in the same boat. For not only linguistics but all other cognitive sciences find the need to postulate a 'level of representations' for mental entities and relations; and, furthermore, doing just that is one of the defining characteristics of a cognitive science.[12]

Both replies show clear signs of epistemological desperation. In the former case, invoking a prior 'language of thought' to accommodate 'representations' of linguistic rules is either regressive or merely metaphorical. It is regressive if this 'language of thought' in turn has rules, which in turn require 'representations'. It is a merely metaphorical solution if this is not the case, since *ex hypothesi* the 'language of thought' then turns out not to be a language. (Appeal to computer analogies will not help here, since the question-begging expression *computer language* is itself an example of the same metaphor.) As for waving the brave banner of 'cognitive science', it will be Job's comfort for linguists to be allowed to join in waving it if what that means is admitting that they do not understand the theoretical foundations of their own discipline, which now turns out to be as suspect as any other which deals in 'mental representations'. (Sounder advice would be just to stop dealing in 'mental representations' and start dealing with language again. It was, after all, being dealt with long before linguistic rules started needing mysterious 'representational' correlates in the brain.)

The epistemological desperation of the 'representationalists' could be probed much further, but to do so here would doubtless smack of sadism. Presumably, 'representational' extremists

---

[11] J.A.Fodor, *The Language of Thought*, New York 1975.
[12] Gardner, op. cit., pp.38ff.

could just dispense with rules altogether, provided they retained neural 'representations' (now 'representing' nothing) which did all the mechanical triggering work necessary to equip the language-user with a 'knowledge' of Russian (or whatever other language is deemed to be 'known'). Such Byzantine theoretical refinements need not concern us either. What needs to be noted at this point is an equivocation which the whole anti-prescriptivist programme has now surreptitiously managed to legitimise through its own metalinguistic takeover of 'rules' from the prescriptivists. Neither 'representationalists' (who hold that linguistic rules or their 'representations' are somewhere in the brain/mind) nor 'equationists' (who hold that 'rules *are* the language'), nor theorists who subscribe to some combination of these two theses, can in principle afford to deny the distinction between (i) rules and (ii) rule-formulations, because this is not compatible with their own tacit surrogational assumptions. But in practice their manoeuvre against normative grammar allows them to conflate precisely that distinction whenever it suits them. For they have put themselves in a position where they can discuss their own rule-formulations *as if* they were discussing rules. The formulations have become surrogates for the (unobservable) rules which they allegedly express or describe.

The distinction between formulations and what they express is a general distinction which has to be respected, regardless of whether we are dealing with grammar or greengrocery. Without that distinction all attempts to make sense of rules break down. (For instance, *No smoking* and *Défense de fumer* are two different formulations of the same rule. A third one might be a red circle enclosing a drawing of a lighted cigarette and a diagonal line through it. Many other formulational possibilities may be envisaged.) Nor is the validity of the distinction affected by the fact that the word *rule* may in certain cases be applied indifferently either to the formulation or to what the formulation expresses. On the contrary, that makes it all the more essential, particularly where language is concerned, to discriminate carefully between the two.

Philosophers who make the general claim that a rule simply 'reduces to' its formulations are using Occam's razor to cut the throat of common sense. What perhaps gives rise to the conviction that rules, unlike formulations, are questionable Platonic abstractions is that legal disputes commonly arise over particular words and phrases in legislative acts and statutes. In many such cases it might seem to follow from the dispute itself that no one is quite sure what rule has been laid down, or whether any rule has been laid down at all. And since any verbal formulation whatever could conceivably be open to dispute of this kind, one might by generalisation of the problem conclude that rules are ontologically superfluous. For, it might be urged, invoking rules ultimately must come down to invoking specific formulations and their (possible) interpretations. However, to argue along these lines in support of the thesis that a rule 'reduces to' its formulations would be to overlook the fact that legal dispute about words or phrases has to be conducted in a particular way in order to qualify as dispute about what the rule is (rather than dispute about any other semantic issue which might be raised in connexion with the words or phrases in question). Recognition of this characteristic form of dispute would itself validate the distinction between rules and formulations, even if nothing else did. The answer to anyone who maintains that looking for a rule over and above its formulations is like looking for an 'Adam-style chair over and above any examples of Adam-style chairs',[13] is to point out that whereas it is impossible to sit in an Adam-style chair without sitting in any particular example of an Adam-style chair, it is perfectly possible to follow a rule without following any particular formulation of it. The reductionist must find it very difficult to see the force of objecting to certain rule-formulations that they misrepresent the rule. Thus, for instance, what is wrong with 'In England drivers must keep to the right-hand side of the road' is that the rule of the road in England is not that. Nevertheless, 'In England drivers must keep to the right-hand side of the road' is clearly recognisable as a rule-formulation: otherwise the objection 'That is not the rule of the road in England' would have no point.

All this is plain enough and requires no recondite hermeneutics. It would hardly be worth stating, were it not that linguistic theorists have claimed for themselves the astonishing right to disregard the distinction in question whenever they wish. This is explained away as being the legitimate use of a 'systematic ambiguity'. Thus, for example,

---

[13] J.S.Ganz, *Rules: a Systematic Study*, The Hague 1971, p.8.

We use the term 'grammar' with a systematic ambiguity. On the one hand, the term refers to the explicit theory constructed by the linguist and proposed as a description of the speaker's *competence*. On the other hand, we use the term to refer to this competence itself. The former usage is familiar; the latter, though perhaps less familiar, is equally appropriate.[14]

Although 'perhaps less familiar' in 1968, by 1978 the 'systematic ambiguity' had been incorporated officially into the technical terminology of transformational grammar.[15] As far as linguistic rules are concerned, this is simply a licence to print your own money.

In the worst abuses of this licence we find that what purport to be discussions of rules are in fact discussions of formulations, and the distinction between the two is not even mentioned.[16] Persistent and pervasive conflation of this order, now common in textbooks written for the current generation of students of linguistics, is what underwrites the linguistic equation 'man = machine'. Once rule-formulations have been passed off as rules of grammar, and rules of grammar in turn misconceived as inhering 'in the language' or else hidden in the brain, the slide down the slope is fast and inevitable. There is nowhere to stop short of construing a theorist's set of rule-formulations as a valid description (at some unspecified 'level of description') of the workings of a linguistic machine. This is the machine of which the human being simply constitutes the physiological frame, with internal rods, pistons and lubrication all provided. It then follows that in order to 'work' linguistically, the human machine needs an 'internal representation' of the rules: and here the computer analogy is brought in to take over. Doubtless it is true that without the advent of the computer it is unlikely that 'grammar' would ever have been defined as 'the set of brain programs by which sentences are generated':[17] but the basic misconception enshrined in this grotesque modern definition is

[14] A.N.Chomsky and M.Halle, *The Sound Pattern of English*, New York 1968, p.3.
[15] J.Ambrose-Grillet, *Glossary of Transformational Grammar*, Rowley 1978, p.52.
[16] e.g. A.N.Chomsky, 'On the notion "rule of grammar" ', *Proceedings of the Twelfth Symposium in Applied Mathematics*, 1961. Reprinted in J.A.Fodor and J.J.Katz (eds.), *The Structure of Language*, Englewood Cliffs 1964.
[17] J.Z.Young, *Programs of the Brain*, Oxford 1979, p.293.

already implicit in the muddle about linguistic rules which ensued from the attempt to make originally prescriptive formulations descriptively respectable.

Finally, we may note the connexion between this conflation and another already encountered, which is intrinsic to the concept of 'computer languages'. It is the assimilation of a set of rules to a causally efficacious mechanism.[18] This takes us back to Turing and his test. It will be recalled[19] that the concept of a rule which was central to Turing's account of computation, and the analogy between the human being's 'book of rules' and the computer's 'table of instructions' depended on a one-way transference of ideas from the human domain to the non-human. That transference will not serve the purposes of Turing's demonstration adequately without the proviso that (some) human rules automatically determine (some features of) the eventual course of human conduct. That is why Turing has to add the qualification that the human being in his comparison 'has no authority to deviate from them in any detail'. It is in this sense that the only rules Turing is interested in are 'fixed rules':[20] he needs the concept of an unbreakable rule – a rule which human beings have no option but to obey.

That is precisely the 'compulsion' which attaches to linguistic rules once they are misconceived in the ways already examined above. To envisage a grammar as a 'device' which 'generates' sentences is already to invite or subscribe to a misunderstanding of what a rule is. Rules generate nothing. Calling them 'generative rules' does not alter that fact (although it may mislead the naive). Nor does Turing's talk about the machine's 'table of instructions' mean that the machine obeys instructions. What is significant, nevertheless, is that the term *rule* tends to be used nowadays in explaining the workings of highly complex electronic machines. No one apparently used to find it necessary to talk of rules in explaining the design of more humdrum, old-fashioned devices such as windmills, or clocks and watches of the pre-digital era. As soon as what a machine does is compared to following rules, we are already half way to accepting that a machine may not be so different from a human being after all. And if we are taught at the same time to believe that linguistic

---

[18] Baker and Hacker, op. cit., pp.281ff.
[19] See above, Introduction.   [20] Turing, op. cit., p.8.

rules are rules we have no option but to obey, we are half way to accepting that a human being is not so different from a machine either. And as long as we continue to decontextualise both language and machines by considering both in abstraction from the social world in which they function, we shall convince ourselves that we have discovered a profound truth. Instead of which, we shall have been taken in by the most bloated of the twentieth century's *idola fori*.

Chapter Seven

Ghosts and Machines

Ryle's famous aphorism describing the human mind according to Descartes as 'the ghost in the machine' has thus been given a new twist by developments in modern linguistic theory. The cognitive ghost itself now turns out to have a machine inside it: a language machine. But this machine in turn has all the attributes of ghostliness. It is a machine that excites rumours and speculations, but no one has ever managed to get an undisputed sighting of it. Accounts of what it looks like are mutually inconsistent. Its spectral presence is invoked to give explanations of supposedly mysterious 'happenings' which would otherwise go unexplained. Its very elusiveness clearly exerts a strong fascination for those who believe in its existence.

Anyone interested in the psychology either of 'ghost-in-the-machine' explanations or of 'machine-in-the-ghost' explanations would do well to ponder Rom Harré's account of an episode in Indian social history:

> When Abdul Khayyum began public bus services to remote areas of the North-West Frontier province certain mullahs objected on the ground that the absence of horses drawing the vehicles implied the presence of djinns under the bonnet. They were induced to withdraw their objections by being shown the actual mechanism by which buses were propelled.[1]

Harré claims that this story illustrates a fundamental principle of scientific theory construction:

> If you don't know why certain things happen, then invent a mechanism (in accordance with the view you take of how the

[1] Harré, op. cit., p.18.

138

world works) – but it is better still if you can find out how nature
really works.[2]

Whether that *is* the lesson which the story of Abdul
Khayyum's bus service teaches us seems doubtful. Lifting the
bonnet is not giving an explanation of the internal combustion
engine. The mullahs relinquished their djinn hypothesis far too
readily. One suspects they may not have believed in djinns in the
first place, but were making a point about the power structure of
local society (namely, that introducing a bus service required the
approval of the appropriate spiritual authority). For if anyone is
intent on maintaining a 'ghost-in-the-machine' theory, there is
simply nothing anyone else can point out about the observable
physical world which will demonstrably prove it wrong. Lifting
the bonnet would be a futile gambit. A resolute mullah can
always postulate djinns inside the carburettor.

Much the same goes for 'machine-in-the-ghost' theories. It will
be of no avail to point out to the true believer that a
species-specific piece of computational equipment enabling
homo sapiens to construct complex grammatical rules but
mutually unintelligible languages would hardly be the most
useful biological endowment in the struggle for survival, and that
making adjectives agree with nouns will not have fed many
mouths or fended off many predators in the course of evolution.
No point that can be made about the conceptual confusion and
explanatory vacuity of 'language machine' hypotheses will oblige
anyone to abandon them who has no intention of doing so. Had
that been the objective of the preceding chapters, it would have
been an objective doomed to failure in advance. To call in
question the theoretical foundations of modern linguistics would
hardly be a worthwhile goal either, being only too easy to
achieve. Modern linguistics, for all its current academic prestige,
has never had theoretical foundations except the very shakiest.
No surveyor's report is needed to call attention to the cracks and
weaknesses in those foundations: they are visible to the naked
eye if anyone cares to look. But that will be no cause for concern
as long as the academic property market continues to boom and
even the most jerrybuilt houses still fetch inflated prices.

The mythology of the language machine will continue to

[2] ibid.

flourish in the foreseeable future, and will continue to impress a public already promised talking bus-stops and instantaneous telephonic translation. But it will flourish – as it flourishes now – at a certain social cost, which is already being paid. The cost is high but gives rise to few public complaints because, rather like the squandering of natural resources, it is an 'invisible' cost borne by the community as a whole.

*   *   *

That theorists of modern linguistics saw themselves from the outset at cross purposes with practitioners of normative grammar is not just a curious item of local history for the chroniclers of language studies. The underlying conflict is between a profoundly amoral view of language and a profoundly moral one. For traditional grammar, whatever its shortcomings and demerits, was ultimately based on an essentially moral view of language. That is rarely if ever emphasised by historians of the Western grammatical tradition: it deserves saying at least once. Traditional prescriptivism does not accept the implied ideological inertia of Saussure's categorical distinction between 'internal' and 'external' linguistics. On the contrary, its own educational theory and practice is implicitly based on a rejection of any such separation. Language is recognised as an essential part of the moral fabric of society. No one who reads Quintilian can be in any serious doubt on this score: grammar and good behaviour are both taught by example, and their teaching is interwoven. Nor did it seem other than obvious to Archbishop Trench in the nineteenth century that 'man starts with language as God's perfect gift, which he only impairs and forfeits by sloth and sin', and that 'with every impoverishing and debasing of personal or national life there goes hand in hand a corresponding impoverishment and debasement of language'.[3] Neither Quintilian's opinions nor the Archbishop's will appeal to everyone, but what cannot be gainsaid is that they reflect a belief that language is far from being just a biological tool available for purposes of communication.

There are many reasons for disagreeing with the assumptions about linguistic authority which traditional grammar promotes, and for questioning the ways in which the linguistic authority

[3] Trench, op. cit., Ch.1.

institutionalised by traditional grammar was wielded. But modern linguistic theory does not propose a more comprehensive analysis of these complexities: instead, it proposes no analysis at all. As soon as one accepts with Saussure and the cyberneticians that linguistic communication is just a matter of sending units of information round a circuit, and that the essence of the linguistic act is captured in observing the operation of this circuit by two anonymous individuals sending each other unspecified verbal messages, then in effect one has already excluded as a theoretical impossibility that linguistic analysis should ever require the recognition of *linguistic* roles other than 'sender' and 'receiver'. Furthermore, even these two roles are linguistically straitjacketed. The only scope which the sender-receiver relationship allows is the choice of which string of words to pass round the circuit. To call the exercise of *this* choice 'rule-governed creativity', as some theorists do, is to parody creativity out of all recognition.

The plea that anything 'else' in language can always be dealt with under some marginal rubric (such as 'sociolinguistics', or 'language use', or 'communicative competence', or 'speech act theory', or any other version or subdivision of Saussure's 'external linguistics') is a plea which itself begs the central question at issue. By marginalising everything 'else', linguistic theory implicitly makes very strong claims which are in no way ideologically inert when they are presented as the only 'scientifically' valid way of looking at language. For the items thus marginalised are the *sine qua non* of language.

Those varieties of 'external linguistics' which concede their own externality by assuming 'that there is for each language-community a given grammar which pre-exists social processes'[4] simply reinforce the dominant language-machine paradigm. Those objecting find themselves trapped in an argument couched in terms drawn from the very same neutralising discourse which decreed their externality in the first place.

This is not to say that the construction of this discourse is confined to or even originates within linguistics. It is a process with many ramifications, some of which happen to be more clearly visible in linguistics than elsewhere. However, these

[4] R.Fowler and G.Cress, 'Critical Linguistics', *Language and Control*, ed. R.Fowler, B.Hodge, G.Cress and T.Trew, London 1979, p.189.

142   *II. The Machine Without*

assume particular importance once society is persuaded to look to the collective expertise of its linguists for an authoritative view of language.

* * *

Pierre Bourdieu[5] points out that any form of linguistic theorising which constantly refers to a monolithic abstraction called simply *la langue* (or something equally vague, such as 'English' or 'French') is already on the side of officialdom in promoting a socio-political idealisation. What is thus reinforced is the view that there is only one legitimate form of language for any given community. It is no mitigation *then* to talk of 'dialects', 'sub-dialects', 'varieties', etc.; for these have already been marginalised at a single initial stroke.

Moreover, this has been achieved without overtly passing judgment on the forms of speech or writing involved. There is no use of crudely pejorative terms such as 'sloppy', 'careless', 'lazy', 'ignorant', 'coarse', 'rustic', 'uncultured' or 'vulgar'. These and their ilk modern linguistics on the whole takes great care to eschew, in order to avoid the banal charge of prescriptivism which it is fond of levelling at traditional grammar.

But what exactly are the social implications when a linguistic theorist (not a normative grammarian) pronounces *They likes she* to be ungrammatical in English? (And, moreover, cites this example to show that although the grammatical structure of English may not be entirely determinate, at least there is a central core which is determinate and about which there can be no disagreement?[6]) It is difficult to see that this pronouncement is not an 'authoritative' downgrading of the English used by native speakers for whom this is a perfectly familiar type of sentence (since, although they would doubtless not describe it in these terms themselves, their singular verb forms all have *-s* inflexions and they use nominative pronouns as direct objects). Can one downgrade people's English without downgrading *them*?

Let us be clear that the question is not whether the individual linguistic theorist has an irrational prejudice against people who

[5] P.Bourdieu, *Ce que parler veut dire*, Paris 1982, p.27.
[6] J.Lyons, *Introduction to Theoretical Linguistics*, Cambridge 1968, p.154.

say 'They likes she', regards them as ignorant, wishes to hold them up to ridicule, etc. Doubtless he can be absolved on all such counts. Nevertheless, *any* categorisation of usage into 'grammatical' and 'ungrammatical' involves a social value judgment of some kind, and it is idle to pretend otherwise. The issue cannot be fudged by concocting outlandish examples of ungrammaticality which people fail to identify as reflecting features of their own usage. Nor can the theoretical point be saved by substituting for *They likes she* an example such as *Splenic why the*, because ungrammaticality is not the same as verbal mishmash. Stringing words together at random in a senseless manner does not involve breaking any rule of grammar, any more than pushing a pawn aimlessly to and fro across a chessboard involves breaking any rule of chess.

Moreover, when the point the theorist wishes to make is quite explicitly that *They likes she* is one of the combinations of English words 'which all linguists will characterise immediately not only as unacceptable, but also as "ungrammatical" ',[7] he is invoking the collective expertise of the whole profession as authority for what he says. It will be of no avail to protest against the downgrading by saying 'But I'm a native speaker of English'. Combinations like *They likes she*, we are informed, 'infringe principles of such generality in standard English that any grammar would necessarily have to take account of them'.[8] So, native speaker or no, your English just is not 'standard English'. The downgrading is official, protest though you may. (You could also protest at the same time that where these 'principles of generality' come from is not at all clear, and that linguistic theorising which fails to make this clear has failed to establish its own validity.)

The social marginalisation to which Bourdieu draws our attention has an interesting extension which involves this controversial word 'standard'. In recent years linguists have discovered 'standards' never heard of before. There is nowadays not only *standard English* but *Welsh Standard English, Scottish Standard English*, and even *Educated Scottish Standard English*. There is *London Regional Standard*, which is different from *Standard English English*. This last would certainly have

[7] ibid.
[8] ibid.

puzzled the Victorians who originally promoted the concept of 'standard English'. They might well have pointed out that an endless proliferation of 'standards' simply makes nonsense of the notion. (To admit a plurality of varieties on an equal footing is, *prima facie*, to deny that there is any standard; for exactly the same reason that the mile is *not* a standard measure of distance if it varies in length from one part of the country to another.) The relevant point here, however, is that this latter-day multiplication of recognised 'standard' varieties of English is itself evidence that 'non-standard' speech is negatively valued. At the same time, it would be naive to suppose that the qualification of the term *standard* by specifying a geographical area is devoid of any social significance. Titular concessions to local pride, the granting of limited measures of regional autonomy, etc. are quite typical signs that the effective social processes of centralisation and unification are already complete. Giving terminological recognition to more and more regions as having linguistic 'standards' of their own is a backhanded way of making clear their subordinate status in relation to a recognised national standard.

If multiplying 'standards' evades the issue, an evasion on an even grander scale is perpetrated by theorists who claim that the basic social unit of language is the 'idiolect'. An idiolect is defined as 'the linguistic system of an individual speaker': a 'personal dialect'.[9] Hence 'idiolectology', if we may call it that, is a variety of linguistic theorising which purports to explain languages in terms of the 'grammars' of individual speakers. The idiolectologist makes a theoretical virtue out of claiming that so-called 'languages' are merely constructs arrived at by generalisation over many individual 'grammars':

> the notion 'language', if it is even coherent, is at a much higher level of abstraction from actual mechanisms than grammar. Grammars exist in the world, as components of steady states attained. As for languages, one may perhaps think of them as determined by grammars, or in some other way, but in any event they are clearly at a further remove from real mechanisms of the brain than the grammars represented in these mechanisms.[10]

[9] D.Crystal, *A Dictionary of Linguistics and Phonetics*, 2nd ed., Oxford 1985, p.152.

[10] A.N.Chomsky, 'Knowledge of language: its elements and origins'. In H.C.Longuet-Higgins, J.Lyons and D.E.Broadbent (eds.), *The Psychological Mechanisms of Language*, London 1981, pp.232-3.

The truth of the matter is just the reverse. 'Idiolects' are theoretical constructs derived from 'languages': they are the individual's private version of the community's system. But once 'real mechanisms of the brain' are identified as the site of 'grammars', while 'languages' are simultaneously dismissed as (dubious) extrapolations therefrom, it becomes as pointless to look for any moral linguistic dimension as it would be, say, in the case of meteorological extrapolations from the readings taken of particular thermometers and barometers. Furthermore, since the idiolectologists, as Nigel Love observes,[11] in practice make no attempt to tackle the theoretical task they have set themselves of recording the several thousand million individual 'grammars' of a 'language' such as 'English', there is no hope of investigating the status of the extrapolation further. Language is thus doubly divorced from social values: (i) by a reductionism which treats only individual brain mechanisms as ultimately 'real', and (ii) by the practical impossibility of obtaining scientifically accurate 'readings' at the 'real' level. Idiolectology bypasses the problem of value judgment involved in setting up standards by the theoretical expedient of allocating to the usage of every individual a standard of its own.

*   *   *

The availability of a neutralising metalanguage also makes it possible to deny that given linguistic usages have any ideological implications at all. A case which has aroused contemporary grammatical controversy is that of gender. It is a particularly interesting controversy because there is no conflict of linguistic evidence: what is at issue is the status of linguistic 'facts'.

In the past, as Deborah Cameron notes,[12] grammarians did not scruple to admit as an obvious linguistic 'fact' that gender distinctions in the Western tradition between 'masculine' and 'feminine' arise, as the terms themselves would seem to indicate, from an assumed correlation with sex. Nor did they scruple to admit that gender systems distinguishing 'masculine' from

[11] N.Love, 'Making sense of Chomsky's revolution', *Language & Communication*, vol.1, 1981, pp.275-87.
[12] D.Cameron, 'What has gender got to do with sex?', *Language & Communication*, vol.5, 1985, pp.19-27.

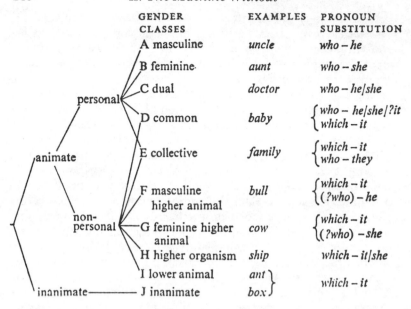

GENDER CLASSES	EXAMPLES	PRONOUN SUBSTITUTION
A masculine	*uncle*	*who – he*
B feminine	*aunt*	*who – she*
C dual	*doctor*	*who – he/she*
D common	*baby*	*who – he/she/?it* / *which – it*
E collective	*family*	*which – it* / *who – they*
F masculine higher animal	*bull*	*which – it* / *(?who) – he*
G feminine higher animal	*cow*	*which – it* / *(?who) –she*
H higher organism	*ship*	*which – it/she*
I lower animal	*ant*	*which – it*
J inanimate	*box*	

(tree: animate → personal {A, B, C, D}, non-personal {E, F, G, H, I}; inanimate → J)

'feminine' in various languages reflected certain assumptions about the social role of women: on the contrary, they explained certain features of these systems by reference to the inequality of the sexes. By contrast, modern linguistics prefers to discuss gender in terms of the workings of syntactic machinery. This by implication denies any direct correlation between gender and sex, and accords no explanatory role to social beliefs about sex differences. The effect of this is to pre-empt any serious argument about the social rights and wrongs connected with gender, by suggesting that it is not scientific to treat the linguistic distinctions involved as being other than merely mechanical. To insist otherwise can easily be made to look like a simple-minded confusion based on equating the term 'masculine' with 'male' and the term 'feminine' with 'female'.

How the neutralising discourse operates in this particular instance may be illustrated by reference to gender in English. There are two official versions of the 'facts', depending on which authorities one consults. Some analyses of English grammar set up highly complex gender classifications, and even more complex rules of syntax to operate with them. Thus the *Grammar of Contemporary English* by Quirk, Greenbaum,

Leech and Svartvik recognises no less than ten genders for English, exemplified by the words *uncle, aunt, doctor, baby, family, bull, cow, ship, ant and box.* These ten different genders are determined on the basis of ten different syntactic patterns, depending on the accompanying pronouns and relatives, as summarised in the table above.[13]

Such a classification in effect redefines the terms *masculine* and *feminine* in terms of syntactic properties and thus by implication rules any question of social bias in the linguistic system out of court. ('How could a rule of syntax be biassed?')

Alternatively, the linguistic theorist may simply deny that a language like English has grammatical gender at all,[14] and explain the uses of its nouns and pronouns as determined simply by 'sex reference' or 'animacy reference' (that is, by objective criteria inhering in the persons and things referred to, and thus 'outside' the linguistic system as such). This involves sweeping under the linguistic carpet a few odd 'exceptions' such as the use of *it* to refer to babies, and the use of *she* to refer to ships, together with a few odd biological riddles such as the status of viruses; but these cases are held not to affect the validity of the general principle.

Both versions of the linguistic 'facts' are called in question by some of the examples Cameron cites from recent newspapers:

(i) *The lack of vitality is aggravated by the fact that there are so few able bodied young adults about. They have all gone off to work or look for work, leaving behind the old, the disabled, the women and the children.*

(ii) *A coloured man subjected to racial abuse went berserk and murdered his next door neighbour's wife with a machete, Birmingham Crown Court heard today.*

(iii) *Fourteen people, three of them women, were arrested.*

The interesting point here is that according to both the theorists who accept and the theorists who deny the existence of grammatical gender in English, the nouns *adult, neighbour* and *people* fall into the class for which the alleged gender is 'common' or the alleged sex-reference indeterminate. Adults,

---

[13] R.Quirk, S.Greenbaum, G.Leech and J.Svartvik, *A Grammar of Contemporary English*, London 1972, p.187.

[14] F.R.Palmer, *Grammar*, 2nd ed., Harmondsworth 1984, pp.195-6.

neighbours and people, we are told, can be either male or female. But when we look at these examples we detect a covert communicational assumption that these nouns will refer to males, except where indicated to the contrary: they are 'crypto-masculines' in current English usage. Anyone who doubts this might reflect on the likelihood of finding in an English newspaper the sentence *Fourteen people, three of them men, were arrested*; or consider how curious examples (i) and (ii) would sound if the words *men* and *husband* were substituted for *women* and *wife* respectively.

Such cases, it should be noted, cannot be explained away by assimilating them to examples like *doctor, professor* and *soldier*, where the assumption that the individuals in question will be males is often 'justified' by reference to the fact that, until relatively recently, only men ever became doctors, professors or soldiers. For it can hardly be supposed that there is, or ever was, an occupational barrier preventing females from becoming adults, neighbours or people.

It is difficult to avoid the conclusion that there is something suspect about any form of linguistic analysis which systematically ignores these patterns of usage and their ideological implications, while purporting to give an objective description of the linguistic 'facts'. Feyerabend may be right to insist that 'facts are constituted by older ideologies';[15] but they may also be constituted as cover-ups for current ideologies too.

*   *   *

No less instructive is the way in which contemporary theorists analyse those areas of linguistic behaviour which appear to involve deliberate and overt moral commitment by the participants themselves. This is the case over a wide range of the linguistic behaviour dealt with by modern 'speech act theory'. A classic example is Searle's analysis of the speech-act of 'promising'.

Such acts are treated as examples of rule-governed linguistic behaviour, but the rules in question are treated as analogous to the rules of games. This analogy is of far-reaching significance. The rules governing games specify necessary and sufficient

---

[15] P.Feyerabend, *Against Method*, London 1975, p.55.

conditions applying to the key features of the game in question. For example, the rules of Association Football specify *inter alia* what constitutes a goal; but they do not specify any particular procedure for enabling you to score one, except, self-evidently, that you must do whatever is necessary in the match you are playing to bring about the satisfaction of those conditions specified for a goal. Nor do such rules lay on you any obligation to attempt to score one, either in general or in specified circumstances. (Rules of the Association Football variety are sometimes called 'constitutive rules', in order to distinguish them from merely 'regulative rules' of the Highway Code variety.)

Searle's rules for promising are given below.[16] There are five of them. They are ordered, and they are couched in terms of what Searle called a promise 'function-indicating' device, designated *Pr*. *Pr* is a form of words to be uttered by the person making the promise, and these rules are the 'semantical rules' for its use.

Rule 1. *Pr* is to be uttered only in the context of a sentence (or larger stretch of discourse) the utterance of which predicates some future act *A* of the speaker *S*.

Rule 2. *Pr* is to be uttered only if the hearer *H* would prefer *S*'s doing *A* to his not doing *A*, and *S* believes *H* would prefer *S*'s doing *A* to his not doing *A*.

Rule 3. *Pr* is to be uttered only if it is not obvious to both *S* and *H* that *S* will do *A* in the normal course of events.

Rule 4. *Pr* is to be uttered only if *S* intends to do *A*.

Rule 5. The utterance of *Pr* counts as the undertaking of an obligation to do *A*.

Rules 2-5 apply only if rule 1 is satisfied, and rule 5 applies only if rules 2 and 3 are satisfied as well.

The details of Searle's rules do not matter for purposes of the present discussion, but what does matter is the whole conception of the explanatory enterprise. There are three salient points about this which call for comment.

Here we see the speech-act theorist proposing a general form of explanation which is obviously intended to be applicable to *all* speech acts. The individual sets of rules will be different, clearly,

---

[16] J.R.Searle, *Speech Acts*, Cambridge 1969, p.63.

in different cases. The rules for promises will not do for greetings. Nevertheless, some such set of rules must be found for greetings too if 'greeting' is to count as a speech act within the terms of the theory (as Searle evidently intends).[17] Unless the theory had this degree of generality, presumably, it would be presumptuous to call it a theory of speech acts at all. Yet this apparently casual assumption of explanatory generality itself conceals a premiss which is by no means ideologically innocent, particularly when combined with a rules model which is manifestly a games model. The games analogy may not always be inappropriate, but it may not always be appropriate either. Greetings, toasts, congratulations, and many other quasi-ritualistic public performances with words may perhaps plausibly be construed as just self-contained verbal games with their own 'constitutive rules'. But once moral acts like promising are not only brought under the same theoretical umbrella but actually cited as paradigm examples, something very curious indeed is going on. A theory which can without batting an academic eyelid subsume greeting and promising under the same explanatory schema is either extremely disingenuous or else it rests upon a general thesis about social action and ethics which needed to be brought out into the daylight and argued for *before* the analysis was proposed. It will not do to shrug this off afterwards, as Searle does ('I think, incidentally, that the obligation to keep a promise probably has no necessary connexion with morality'[18]), for by then the neutralising discourse of rule-formulation has established its own rhetorical momentum, and that rhetoric automatically marginalises the question of whether any given speech act has a 'connexion with morality'. This becomes an 'external' question, just as for Saussure the question of what *A* and *B* are talking about and who they are become 'external' questions.

The second point is that reference to moral concepts is actually treated by this form of explanation as on a par with reference to psychological phenomena such as preferences and expectations (see Rules 2 and 3). For all Searle's disclaimers about the dubiety of the connexion between the speech act of 'promising' and morality, we find when we look at his Rule 5 that

---

[17] Searle, op. cit., pp.64-5.
[18] Searle, op. cit., p.188.

making sense of this rule involves making sense of 'the undertaking of an obligation'. At this point there surfaces a crypto-behaviourism which Searle would doubtless be the first to repudiate. The repudiation stands only at the expense of committing the rules for promising to a moral regress. In other words, what constitutes a promise is now explained by appeal to a moral concept ('obligation') which itself has no explanation in terms of speech-act rules. A theorist who desperately wanted to could probably plug that hole by setting up 'obligation' as a speech act in its own right. By some such strategy it might be possible to rule moral concepts out of the reckoning altogether, by providing always a reference back to particular types of speech act. One might even applaud such theoretical ingenuity if one thought that circularity was the hallmark of successful explanation.

The third point involves consideration of a different circularity. For the speech-act theorist, linguistic behaviour is essentially communicative behaviour. Thus promising, greeting, etc. are all acts of linguistic communication. ('In speaking a language I attempt to communicate things to my hearer by means of getting him to recognize my intention to communicate just those things.'[19]) However, the five rules for promising do not in themselves tell us what form of words *Pr* actually is or might be. This in itself seems to leave an unsatisfactory gap in the account. If I have to make a promise in Spanish, it is not much use my knowing merely the general conditions which have to be satisfied for promising if I am going to put my foot in it by employing, say, the literal translation of an English 'promising' formula which turns out to be an idiomatic insult in Spanish. This gap is bridged in Searle's analysis by appeal to a quite different set of rules, 'the semantical rules of the dialect spoken by *S* and *H*'. So *in order* to engage in this (*pace* Searle) moral act at all, it turns out that the speaker and hearer have to be both members of a Saussurean linguistic community, where the socio-political idealisation of linguistic uniformity already holds by theoretical fiat. Only thus can difficulties about 'understanding' one's moral commitment be theorised out of existence. No one can complain about the elegance of making the rules for the function-indicating device *Pr* depend on the condition that 'the

---

[19] Searle, op. cit., p.43.

sentence uttered is one which, by the semantical rules of the language, is used to make a promise'. The only trouble with this elegance is that now we have come back to our starting point. Was not making a promise precisely the notion we originally set out to explicate?

Once again, somehow or other, the moral dimension of language has vanished into thin air, and we are left with a machinery of linguistic rules instead.

*   *   *

Marcuse comments perceptively on the way in which twentieth-century 'ordinary language philosophy' with its *There's-a-bittern-at-the-bottom-of-the-garden* examples manages to reduce what is multi-dimensional to just a single dimension.[20] He does not, however, appear to sense the connexion between this and the even more striking dimensional shrinkage of modern linguistics. Once linguistic theory, by decontextualising language, insists on reduction to a single plane of 'form', a single plane of 'meaning', and a single scale of 'grammaticality', whole landscapes of linguistic nuance have already been flattened out by descriptive bulldozing. The resultant levelling is intimately related to the philosopher's 'sterilized and anesthetized' samples of speech which Marcuse criticises.

Ordinary language philosophy needed a morally anaesthetised concept of 'correct' usage as its starting point, and it is no mere coincidence that the rise of British ordinary language philosophy coincided with the most elaborate attempt ever made to standardise the English language and provide a historical validation for sanctioned usage. This dependence is plainly visible in the case of the founder of ordinary language philosophy, G.E.Moore. His work is particularly interesting because one of its main concerns, from the publication of *Principia Ethica* in 1903, was moral theory.

Moore's moral theorising rested on the notion that 'the language' had already established the meanings of words like *good* and *bad*, and that these meanings were known to everyone who knew how to use such words 'correctly'. Moore strenuously

[20] H.Marcuse, *One-Dimensional Man*, London 1964, Ch.7.

denied that his own use of ethical vocabulary was in any way theoretically question-begging:

> *Principia* does not use the words 'good', 'right', 'ought', 'duty' in any sense other than the one in which they are used in common speech; and hence there is no such thing as a 'notion of duty' which is peculiar to *Principia*, in the sense that it is a notion for which the word 'duty' stands in *Principia* but for which it does not stand in ordinary speech ... All that I did was to make propositions *about* the ordinary senses of those words, *not* to introduce new senses.[21]

Moore sometimes speaks of the 'ordinary sense' of an expression, sometimes of its 'standard English meaning', and sometimes of the 'best English usage', but without appearing to distinguish between these or to question whether they are objectively 'given' as linguistic facts. He explains what he means by the 'correct' use of an expression as follows:

> Suppose it were true (a) that the best English usage is such that a man will be using the words 'It was wrong of Brutus to stab Caesar' correctly, i.e. in accordance with the best English usage, if and only if he means by them neither more nor less than that he himself, at the time of speaking, disapproves of this action of Brutus'; and that hence he will be using them *both* correctly *and* in such a way that what he means by them is *true*, if and only if, at the time when he says them, he does disapprove of this action. (Of course, a man may be using a sentence perfectly correctly, even when what he means by it is *false*, either because he is lying or because he is making a mistake; and similarly, a man may be using a sentence in such a way that what he means by it is *true*, even when he is not using it correctly, as for instance, when he uses the wrong word for what he means, by a slip or because he has made a mistake as to what the correct usage is. Thus using a sentence *correctly* – in the sense explained – and using it in such a way that what you mean by it is *true*, are two things which are completely logically independent of one another: either may occur without the other.)[22]

For any philosopher who takes this position it is clearly crucial to have a clear distinction between 'correct' and 'incorrect' usage, and essential there should be no serious argument about

[21] G.E.Moore, 'A reply to my critics', *The Philosophy of G.E.Moore*, ed. P.A.Schilpp, New York 1952, p.570.
[22] ibid., p.548.

establishing what it is. Furthermore, it would have seemed unnecessary for a philosopher of Moore's generation to doubt the credentials of a concept like 'best English usage', it being taken for granted that this was precisely the national usage being codified by Murray and the Oxford lexicographers. With every volume of the *O.E.D.* that was published, this philosophical position became stronger, in the sense that more and more 'best English usage' was put beyond doubt and given its historical *bona fides*. The dictionary defined not only words like *chair* and *table* but also words like *good, right* and *duty*. It thus supplied the essential empirical support for Moore's claim that his own use of moral terms was objective and unbiassed. Remove that support and the basis of the philosophical position collapses.

Moore's appeals to established usage and to 'common sense' made his philosophical reputation. They extended across a whole range of philosophical topics. Moore's arguments about the nature of perception, for instance, are based on the assumption that when we speak of perceiving physical objects, such as doors or fingers, in many or even most cases 'we are neither using language incorrectly, nor making any mistake about the facts'.[23] As one commentator puts it, 'the essence of Moore's technique of refuting philosophical statements consists in pointing out that these statements *go against ordinary language*'.[24] But as a *philosophical* technique this would certainly have lacked credibility in any earlier age when correct usage was not generally regarded as authoritatively 'fixed'.

Moore is by no means the only British philosopher of the interwar period to situate philosophical problems by reference to a taken-for-granted notion of 'correct' English. In 1936 we find the following paragraph in A.J.Ayer's *Language, Truth and Logic*:

It is misleading, also, to say, as some do, that philosophy tells us how certain symbols are actually used. For this suggests that the propositions of philosophy are factual propositions concerning the behaviour of a certain group of people; and this is not the case. The philosopher who asserts that, in the English language, the sentence 'The author of *Waverley* was Scotch' is equivalent to

[23] N.Malcolm, 'Moore and ordinary language', *The Philosophy of G.E.Moore*, ed. P.A.Schilpp, New York 1952, p.349.
[24] G.E.Moore, 'Some judgments of perception', *Proceedings of the Aristotelian Society*, vol.19, 1918, p.7.

'One person, and one person only, wrote *Waverley*, and that person was Scotch' is not asserting that all, or most, English-speaking people use these sentences interchangeably. What he is asserting is that, in virtue of certain rules of entailment, namely those which are characteristic of 'correct' English, every sentence which is entailed by 'The author of *Waverley* was Scotch', in conjunction with any given group of sentences, is entailed also by that group, in conjunction with 'One person, and one person only, wrote *Waverley*, and that person was Scotch.' That English-speaking people should employ the verbal conventions that they do is, indeed, an empirical fact. But the deduction of relations of equivalence from the rules of entailment which characterize the English, or any other, language is a purely logical activity; and it is in this logical activity, and not in any empirical study of the linguistic habits of any group of people, that philosophical analysis consists.[25]

Here we see a clear division of labour established between the philosopher and the linguist. It is evidently not the philosopher's job to establish what the 'verbal conventions' of the English language are: that is a task for the linguist, and the philosopher simply assumes the linguist's competence to carry it out. Equally, it is not the linguist's job to investigate the 'logic' of English: that is a task to be left to the philosopher. Thus between them philosopher and linguist can analyse the totality of language with complete scientific impartiality since neither is called upon to exercise any *linguistic* value judgment, or to claim a professional expertise which might be disputed by other experts.

The problem with this convenient interdisciplinary 'division of labour' is that although the two parts superficially appear to complement and support each other there is actually an awkward discontinuity separating them. This discontinuity is papered over by the term *correct*. The philosopher assumes that the linguist can supply the details of 'correct usage': but the 'correctness' needed for the philosopher's purposes has to fill the gap in any given instance between getting the facts right and making a true statement of them. It is far from clear, however, that the linguist's 'correct usage' can do this, without opening up a moral dimension to linguistic investigations which both linguist and philosopher are professionally anxious to exclude.

[25] A.J.Ayer, *Language, Truth and Logic*, London 1936, pp.69-70.

There are two sociolinguistic flies in the ointment of 'correct usage'. One is that when correct usage is construed, as it is quite overtly by Moore, as 'best English usage' the question cannot be indefinitely evaded as to whose value judgment about English validates the term 'best'. This is the fly of prescriptivism. The other fly is the fly of dishonesty. The philosopher evidently needs a concept of 'correct usage' which covers lying. Moore, as is evident from his remarks about correctness cited above, is quite willing to allow that whether a person is lying makes no difference to the correctness of the English used. Unfortunately, it *does* make a difference to the investigative concerns of linguists. From the lexicographer's point of view a liar who calls black *white* is just not using the word *white* 'correctly'.

The philosophical notion of 'correct usage' and the linguistic notion of 'correct usage', far from providing mutual comfort and support for each other, are actually at odds. Dishonest informants are of no more use in linguistics than dishonest witnesses are welcome in court.

As if in reaction to this problem, Tarski proposed what he called 'the semantic conception of truth',[26] and postwar semantics followed his lead by endeavouring to build the notion of 'truth' *ab initio* into the notion of 'linguistic meaning'. This is the basis of all varieties of the currently popular academic programme of 'truth-conditional semantics', championed alike by philosophers and linguists. Here we see another ramification of the attempt to divorce language from social morality, and another visitation of the mechanical ghost, which is now credited with the ability to conjure up veracity out of linguistic rules.

The various available versions of truth-conditional semantics differ from one another in ways which do not affect the main point here at issue, for all incorporate the same three basic principles. The first and most fundamental, which might for convenience be called the 'cognitive principle', is that 'to know the meaning of a sentence is to know under what conditions one who utters it says something true'.[27] (Against the objection that many sentences are never normally used to make statements at

[26] A.Tarski, 'The semantic conception of truth', *Philosophy and Phenomenological Research*, vol.4, 1944, pp.341-75.

[27] P.F.Strawson *Meaning and Truth*, Oxford 1970, p.24. For the history of the notion of 'truth conditions', see G.P.Baker and P.M.S.Hacker, *Language, Sense and Nonsense*, Oxford 1984, Ch.4.

all, the cognitive principle is usually defended by arguing that knowing the meaning of interrogative sentences, imperative sentences, etc. can be treated as derivable from or reducible to knowing the meaning of corresponding declaratives. Hence the 'typical' sentence for truth-conditionalists is usually a simple affirmative declarative sentence with the verb in the indicative mood.)

The second principle is that when someone says, for example, 'I am hungry', the statement that person makes has a determinate 'truth value'; namely, that it is true (value T) if indeed the speaker is hungry, but false (value F) if not. This we may call the 'truth determinacy principle'. The simplest system of truth values has just two values (T and F): more complex systems are sometimes invoked, but for present purposes they may be ignored. The truth-determinacy principle envisages the world we live in as consisting of a complex combination of permanent and transitory 'states of affairs', a certain number of which obtain at any given moment. Individual declarative sentences, according to the theory, correspond to states of affairs. They can be used to make a true statement whenever the corresponding state or states of affairs obtain, or to express a falsehood otherwise. A complete and correct description of the world at any time would comprise the total set of sentences corresponding to the state of the world at that time (the various states of affairs then obtaining).

It is held to be no objection to the truth-determinacy principle that people often disagree about 'the facts'. Street accidents and sports furnish countless examples. Did the driver signal too late? Was the centre-forward really offside? Did the batsman play a stroke? Even when all allowances are made for human error and difficulties of observation, a residue of cases will doubtless remain in which unbiassed witnesses with the best of evidence may still be in doubt or divided as to 'what actually happened'. But this would not invalidate the truth-determinacy principle: on the contrary. For if the principle did not hold, there would be nothing to be in doubt or divided about. (In any case, whether an assertion is true or false is not to be confused with whether people are sure or doubtful of its truth. The latter, we are told, are psychological questions, not semantic questions. Nor is the truth to be established in controversial cases by counting heads: that would be to confuse semantics with statistics.) According to truth-conditional theory, therefore, knowing the truth conditions of a declarative sentence enables one in principle to assess the truth value of any statement it is used to make, relative to any given state of the world. In practice, patently, all kinds of factors may intrude to prevent particular individuals from making reliable assessments in particular cases. But then, no one ever supposed that learning English (or any other language) conferred either omniscience or infallibility upon the learner.

The third principle takes one further step. Between them the cognitive principle and the truth-determinacy principle are not adequate to provide a fully satisfactory semantic theory, because equivalence in truth value does not add up to equivalence in meaning. (Thus although, for example, the statements 'The Romans invaded America in 55 BC' and 'The Romans invented the atomic bomb' have never been true and never will be, the two English sentences *The Romans invaded America in 55 BC* and *The Romans invented the atomic bomb* do not mean the same. Yet the two principles so far considered provide no way of distinguishing between them; for under no conditions (past, present or future) obtaining in the world as we know it will the corresponding statements have different truth values.) The move which truth-conditional theory makes in order to circumvent limitations of this kind is to invoke a 'possible worlds principle'. This principle defines truth conditions not by reference to all past, present and future states of the world in which we live, but by reference to 'all possible worlds'. The advantage of this neo-Leibnizian strategy is intended to be that it supplies a way of distinguishing between sentences like *The Romans invaded America in 55 BC* and *The Romans invented the atomic bomb*. For although, in our world, statements to the effect that the Romans invaded America or invented the atomic bomb will always be uniformly false, it is possible – so the argument goes – that world history might have been different. In one possible world it might have been the case that 'The Romans invaded America in 55 BC' was true, for instance, but 'The Romans invented the atomic bomb' false. But in another possible world, the latter statement might have been true and the former false. Thus the 'possible worlds principle' makes it possible to distinguish semantically between the two sentences.

Much ingenuity has been exercised by truth-conditionalists in attempting to show that, on the basis of these three principles, the meanings of all types of sentences must yield eventually to explication along the lines of Tarski's famous example: '*Snow is white' is true if and only if snow is white.*[28] To what extent these attempts can be counted successful is less germane to the present discussion than the epistemological spirit of the whole truth-conditionalist enterprise. Here we see a semantics which not only drains the concept 'truth' of any moral content but divorces statements from their communicational context altogether. For while there is no denying that in everyday life we recognise an important connexion between the meanings of the words people use and the truth or otherwise of what they say, nevertheless to reduce that connexion to a simple correspondence between hypothetical 'states of affairs' and 'sentences' is to misrepresent it entirely. The result is a semantics for robots, not human beings. More exactly, it is language-machine semantics. For the assumption is that in the course of the process of language acquisition our internal cognitive machinery computes a fixed semantic value or values for every expression in the language, and does so solely on the basis of the truth or falsity of the statements those expressions may be used to make.

What is wrong with the scenario of truth-conditional semantics is simple and fundamental. Human beings do not live in the many 'possible worlds' imagined by truth-conditionalists, but in the world of here and now. Whether snow is white in all possible worlds is something most of us do not know, and we do not care either. And while we certainly use the words *true* and *false* in appraising what people say in this here-and-now world, we use those words in evaluations which are in various important respects quite different from the semantic theorist's. Although the truth-conditionalist sets out from what sounds like our everyday notion of truth-appraisal, before long one finds that in order to suit the purposes of semantic theory that notion has been subjected to a drastic and radical oversimplification. At the outset we may well agree that someone 'makes a true statement if and only if things are as, in making that statement, he states them to be'.[29] But that does not commit us to envisaging truth as a straightforward one-one correspondence between what is stated on the one hand and 'how things are' on the other.

[28] Tarski, op. cit.
[29] Strawson, op. cit., p.15.

Untruths are not simply truths which have somehow wandered into the wrong world. In appraising questions of truth and falsehood we ordinarily take into account not only the circumstances of the statement but both the speaker's and hearer's points of view.

True is a word we use primarily to express our agreement with someone else's assessment of a situation or, somewhat differently, to make it clear we do not think that person is lying. The connexion between these uses is not fortuitous. *True* is a word which passes judgment on an individual or a source of information as well as on what was said. The use of *true* does not commit us to standing by what Smith said through thick and thin, come hell or high water: the judgment involved is essentially a context-bound judgment, in the sense that we thereby make no claim to have investigated every shred of evidence before deciding whether or not to express our agreement with what Smith said, and rarely suppose that Smith has either. Our support is support for what Smith said *in a particular communication situation,* given the understood purposes for which the communicational exchange takes place. It is evident that we cannot sensibly agree or disagree with what Smith says without understanding the words Smith uses: but all we need to understand for this is what point Smith's words have for purposes of that situation. Whether what Smith says would hold good next week, next year, or on another planet are alike irrelevances. By saying that what Smith says is true we do not claim it to be an unimpeachable statement that admits no further qualification: we simply affirm our view of its trustworthiness for the purposes in hand. To this extent, we ourselves take responsibility for the trustworthiness of Smith: and thus undertake a moral commitment of our own to any third party involved. The word *true* is also a lexical mark of that commitment.

No such commitment is implied in truth-conditional semantics, where *true* refers to an impersonal idealisation of faultless descriptive accuracy. In a semantic theory where there was no room in the first place for the question 'From whose point of view is the statement true?' there will be no room for an answer, and hence no room either for any interpersonal dimension of meaning. A semantic theory where rules of inference operate in a communicational vacuum, irrespective of who is saying what to whom, for what purposes and in what circumstances, is a semantic theory in which truth has already been anaesthetised, numbed by a massive injection of formal logic.

*   *   *

Truth is not the only casualty once language is reduced to mental mechanisms. Knowledge is automatically devalued along with it. Thus once upon a time anyone would have been ridiculed who maintained that the clock in the town square knows what time it is: on the ground that, other than metaphorically, it makes no sense to attribute propositional knowledge to mechanical contrivances. But when nowadays a leading computer expert solemnly gives it as his view that 'the thermostat thinks the room is too warm in the same sense that a human being might',[30] many will doubtless hesitate before dismissing that as nonsense. The hesitation is revealing. It is not that the humble thermostat nowadays basks in the reflected glory of the computer. What has happened is far more subtle and radical than that. What has changed is not our view of thermostats but our view of language. Propositional knowledge was once held to be impossible without language: so how could a simple thermostat know or believe 'that the room is too warm'? Computer culture stands this reasoning on its head. The words 'the room is too warm' become merely a more mechanically sophisticated series of noises than a simple click which your central heating makes as it switches itself off: a difference in complexity rather than a difference in kind.

Similarly, those who are impressed when a philosopher explains that inside today's computers there are 'self-understanding representations',[31] and nod their heads sagely lest they be thought stupid, are nodding acknowledgment not to the miracles of modern technology but to the triumph of a mechanistic concept of language. A 'self-understanding representation' is presumably a representation that understands itself: hence, knows how to do what it needs to do. And a respresentation must be a symbol of some kind. So a self-understanding representation would be the ultimately

[30] John McCarthy, *Computer Culture*, ed. H.R.Pagels, New York 1984, p.152.
[31] D.C.Dennett, *Computer Culture*, ed. H.R.Pagels, New York 1984, p.272.

autonomous symbol. A long line of philosophers from Hume onwards, we are told,[32] worried needlessly about human knowledge because they failed to grasp the simple fact that there exist representations that understand themselves. Thought and knowledge are no longer mysteries once computer culture has taught us how to extend the autonomy of language to the autonomy of symbolic representation in general.

*   *   *

Developments of the kind discussed above are aberrations which the myth of the language machine unavoidably promotes. Unavoidably, because the workings of the machine are envisaged as totally independent of any criteria or values entertained by the machine's human operators. Thus a form of discourse about language is created which serves either to disengage language from human motives and intentions, or to disguise the extent and nature of that engagement. Through this discourse language is presented as being in itself neutral, a mere communal instrument or facility. Ethical, political and aesthetic judgments are passed only on particular 'uses' of language by particular individuals or groups in particular circumstances. Truth becomes not a social construct but an impersonal correspondence between words and 'reality'. If language has a role, it is always a passive one. ('How could a machine possibly be accountable for what people do with its products?') The myth of the language machine is a convenient myth because it absolves us from our day-to-day duties as language-makers, and blankets out for us all awkward questions concerning the exercise of authority through language. We purchase this linguistic security at cost price: and the cost is the removal of language from the domain of social morality altogether.

[32] ibid., pp.271-2.

Saying Nothing

A   B

'Good morning, B.'

'Good morning, A.'

'What shall we talk about today, B?'

'I've forgotten what it was we were talking about yesterday. But I expect it was the same old grouse.'

'You mean this rotten job we've got?'

'Precisely. Here we are with absolutely no retirement prospects, condemned to appear for ever on page 27 of the *Cours de linguistique générale*, saying nothing.'

'Come now, B. I see you *are* in a bad mood today. I quite agree that being stuck here until kingdom come isn't funny. But why do you say "saying nothing"?'

'Why? Because that's exactly the job description. Or are you going to try to be clever in the way philosophers are and tell me that saying nothing might itself be saying something? Some zero morphemes full of sound and fury, perhaps? Or just the inaudible product of a few deletion rules?'

'Well, B, admittedly there's nothing on page 27 of the *Cours* for us to *say*. But there's something for us to *show*. Isn't our diagram really a way of showing that we can talk about *everything*?'

'Is there a difference, then, between talking about everything and saying nothing?'

163

'Really, B! That's pretty close to linguistic heresy. Are you trying to get us the sack? We of all people know there must be a difference. After all, the word *nothing* isn't the same as the word *something*. That's a fact guaranteed by the linguistic code.'

'But it just isn't true that we can talk about everything. We can only talk about what the linguistic code allows us to talk about.'

'But that's fairly extensive, you must admit.'

'That's not the point. The scope a linguistic code affords us is merely contingent. A code as such can be quite restrictive.'

'I've never felt bothered by that myself.'

'All the same, I wish Bally and Sechehaye had given us *something* to say on page 27.'

'You wish they had provided us with a script?'

'Well, at least it would have been something.'

'My dear B, that is an absolutely absurd suggestion, if I may say so. I think the job must be getting you down after all these years. I know we've been doing it now ever since 1916 without reprieve. But can't you see how much worse it would be if we had a script? We should be condemned to repeat the same thing for ever and ever. Personally, I'd much rather be saying nothing, as you put it, than have what I am to say dictated by a script.'

'So you object to dictation by a script, but not to dictation by a code. I suppose that shows something at least about the way you imagine language works. But you are probably right: a script would get terribly monotonous.'

'It's not just the monotony, B. Don't you see that a script would defeat the whole point of our job?'

'I'm not sure I follow.'

'Now B, when you talk like that you make me wonder whether you have ever really understood what our job is.'

'All right, A. I have a feeling you're going to tell me.'

'You and I have been appointed to this very important and highly responsible position of acting as linguistic representatives for the whole of humanity.'

'Is that why we have to wear these vacant expressions on our faces?'

'Now don't be perverse, B. We certainly weren't selected just because we happen to look like shop-window dummies.'

'Nor because we happen to be white, male, clean-shaven and have neat haircuts?'

'Of course not. You must try to put thoughts like that out of your mind.'

'Then why *were* we selected as linguistic representatives for the whole of humanity?'

'You know that as well as I do, B. We were the only two people Bally and Sechehaye could find who spoke exactly the same language.'

'But if that is so rare, how does it qualify us to represent all humanity? Aren't we just freaks? Surely it would have been more representative to find two people who did *not* speak exactly the same language.'

'Dear me, B. Sometimes I have doubts about your education. Our business is linguistic *science*, not social sampling. Didn't anyone ever teach you anything about the scientific role of idealisation?'

'Yes, I seem to remember they did; but I could never quite grasp it.'

'It's very simple really. This is a ramshackle old universe in which things never actually work as they should. So in order to understand it, scientists have to imagine that everything is working perfectly. That's idealisation.'

'So you are saying that because we happen to speak exactly the same language we embody the ideal conditions for a scientific understanding of language?'

'Exactly!'

'Precisely because that is *not* how language actually works for most people, but how it *ought* to?'

'Now don't twist my words, B.'

'I thought the linguistic code made word-twisting impossible.'

'But I didn't say anything like what you said I said.'

'On the contrary, A. You said something very like that.'

'Let me try to rephrase it then. By speaking exactly the same language we represent an idealisation which allows linguistic scientists to understand what factors in the real world actually prevent perfect linguistic communication from taking place. Saussure, after all, never claimed that linguistic communication was flawless. Clearly, it's not; except for identical twins like us.'

'So, if I now see what you're driving at, A, understanding how language works and how it does not work are two sides of the same coin. And that is where theoretical idealisation comes in. Hence our role.'

'Just so, B. You're quick off the mark today. Linguistic idealisation is absolutely essential if scientists are to understand anything at all about human linguistic skills. And that is both how and why we two stand as linguistic representatives for all our fellow creatures. We actually *constitute* a homogeneous linguistic community.'

'There are still a number of things that worry me about our job, A.'

'What are they?'

'First, who knows that you and I actually *are* speaking exactly the same language?'

'Why *we* do, of course. Don't we?'

'Sometimes I doubt it.'

'But why, B?'

'Perhaps just because I seem to fail to communicate my doubts to you.'

'That's very easily explicable, B. Nowadays linguists all recognise that performance is never an exact reflection of competence. Put your mind at rest on that score.'

'But you said, A, we were an idealisation of the linguistic state of humanity. Ought we not ideally to agree?'

'But we *do*, B. We *do*. You have just agreed with what I said about idealisation. What you call "doubts" about it were just temporary psychological hiccoughs. In the end, we both knew what the word *idealisation* means, didn't we?'

'That's just my question, A. Neither of us was responsible for inventing the word *idealisation*: it belongs to the linguistic code. We're just supposed to have its correct meaning automatically stored in our mental lexicon. But is it? And how would we know?'

'That's silly, B. We know it must be there, because if it weren't there you wouldn't be able to understand me when I used the word *idealisation*, and nor would I be able to understand you when you used the word *idealisation*. You can't retrieve an item of information from a computer's store if the item of information wasn't there in the first place.'

'Beg pardon, A. That just begs my question. What I am asking is whether we *do* understand each other when we use the word *idealisation*. Perhaps we only think we do.'

'Really, B. Now you're just being perverse again. Of course we understand each other, because we speak the same language. What's your next question?'

'Well, if we *are* actually speaking the same language, how on earth did it happen? We are identical twins, and I know we were brought up together. But does that explain it?'

'I grant you the explanation isn't terribly clear in the text we're supposed to illustrate. But of course you must remember that Saussure lived and died before the computer revolution. He didn't really know much about what goes on in the brain. But nowadays scientists know that the human brain is just a computer. What is remarkable is how the computer revolution retrospectively proved Saussure right.'

'In what way, A?'

'Quite simple, my dear B. Nowadays we know – because computer science has actually proved it – that any code can be broken down into simple "yes-or-no" decisions which a machine can handle. So even machines can communicate provided they are programmed in the same way. In other words, what matters is that they are using the same system. But with incompatible systems it's just impossible.'

'So somehow Nature has provided us with internal linguistic machinery that matches up?'

'Ideally, yes. But in practice the matching depends on our being exposed to the same system in the first place. Nature only guarantees that *if* two individuals have the same linguistic upbringing *then* they will internalise the same linguistic code, as we have. But that also explains why neither you nor I understand a word of Tahitian. If you were to attempt linguistic communication with a monolingual speaker of Tahitian it would be like trying to link up machines which have been programmed to operate on quite different circuits. The really important point, though, is that modern technology shows that information *can* be transmitted from one system of machinery to another, provided that at *some* level there is compatibility between equipment. Identity is just a theoretical idealisation of maximum compatibility. That's the ultimate idealisation Saussure went for as regards language; and the subsequent progress of the computer age increases our confidence that he must have been right all along the line.'

'So that explains both why, in principle, any human being can acquire any language, but at the same time why human beings who have in fact learned quite different languages will not understand one another?'

'Full marks, B.'

'But how can we be sure that Nature *did* equip us with this wonderful machinery?'

'Now I've already warned you twice about perversity, B. You *know* that somehow we acquire a linguistic code, because otherwise human beings would be just like pigs or monkeys, bereft of all the benefits of linguistic communication. And if we were thus bereft, how do you explain the fact that the two of us are discussing precisely this topic here and now?'

'I just don't know, A.'

'Precisely. You have no better explanation to propose. Any more questions?'

'It's not a matter of whether *I* have a better explanation than yours, A, but of whether *you* have any explanation at all. Postulating cerebral machinery to do the job Saussure's idealisation requires only makes sense on the assumption that the idealisation was right in the first place. However, I do have one more question.'

'What is that?'

'Because our job is to represent a linguistic idealisation, it doesn't give any scope for linguistic criticism. We are like publicity agents employed to advertise a commercial product, and thereby debarred from questioning whether the product is what the advertisement claims it to be, whether it is right to advertise it, or what the consequences, good or bad, might be.'

'But surely, B, these are moral scruples, not linguistic doubts. Linguistics has nothing to do with morality. It is a science. Every science needs a theoretical foundation. That is precisely what Saussure's idealisation provides for linguistics. And furthermore, if all scientists started having moral scruples about the possibility that their work might be misapplied or misinterpreted, science would just grind to a halt. Our job is to promote the theoretical foundation which linguistic science needs.'

'That's just what worries me, A. Calling something "science" is nowadays one way of insulating it from any criticisms based on social value judgments. Science thinks it can't be called to account except by scientists. Do you think it just doesn't matter if readers who see our two silently talking heads as representative of the human linguistic condition may be misled into a complete misunderstanding of that condition?'

'I don't understand what you are getting at. How can science possibly mislead?'

'The picture of our two talking heads saying nothing surely promotes the idea that what you say and how you say it in the end make little difference, because a scientific understanding of the language is based on abstracting from such particularities. Indeed, if you really want to understand how language works you must first make that abstraction. Here our job seems to be endorsing a concept of linguistic science which is itself highly questionable, because it deliberately seeks to detach language from involvement in human action and human values.'

'By no means, B. It is you who are guilty of distortion. Our job is not to conceal the involvement of language in human action, or to deny that speech in practice entails value judgments. The point is simply that, as regards the theoretical foundations of the science, the specific actions and judgments just don't matter.'

'But that, A, is exactly my point. You repeat it, but you don't seem to get it. Let me try to put it another way.'

'Go on.'

'Would it make any difference if we wrote to the publishers and suggested that in their next reprint of the *Cours* they might update the illustrations, and replace the picture of our two heads by a diagram of two connected office computers exchanging anonymous information along the wires linking them? Or would a machine diagram do just as well to exemplify the theoretical foundations of linguistic science?'

'Just as well, of course. It might even sell a few more copies of the book. But then we should be out of work.'

'Were we ever *in* work? Or were we always just standing in for the language machines of the future?'

'Being a stand-in is a perfectly respectable job in some walks of life. But I am still not sure I understand this prejudice you seem to have against machines.'

'Let me try just once more. Why is it that in our job we never actually *do* anything?'

'*Do* anything? Of course we do. We illustrate the fundamental *modus operandi* of linguistic communication.'

'What I mean, A, is that we're not allowed on page 27 to do anything *except* talk (even if you don't agree with me that we have to talk about nothing and have nothing to say). Can this inactivity possibly represent the idealised human linguistic condition? Is language really a *substitute* for action? Isn't language in real life essentially integrated with all sorts of actions, and inseparable from them? Does it even make sense to think of language as a separate form of activity in the list of human activities?'

'I've answered all this before, B. You're just trying to catch me out. It's not like the case of the king sitting on his throne who, when asked "But what do you *do* all day?", replied, "I reign. That's what I *do*." '

'I'm not at all clear that the king's job was a great deal different from ours in that respect.'

'But we do talk. You cannot deny that. That's what we *do*, and are seen to be doing as representatives of our species. Again, it's like machines. Surely the ideal representation of any given class of machines would be a machine that executed to perfection all and only the operations which such machines are designed for. *Homo loquens*, as we now know, is essentially just a talking machine.'

'But would a machine talk just for the sake of it?'

'If it were so designed!'

'But what would be the point of that?'

'Who knows? Ask the designer. You're just trying to catch me out again, B, aren't you? Now listen to me. Every time you talk to me about the futility of this rotten job we have, you belie your basic contention. The plain fact is that what you say is not just talk. It's the expression of an opinion about your job. So at least this language machinery you are so sceptical about enables you to make value judgments and argue rationally in support of those judgments. What more do you want, for heaven's sake? Not all jobs carry such bonuses.'

'*I* may know that's so. But linguistic science apparently takes no account of it in its theoretical idealisation. What is a value judgment without the possibility of action? We can't go on strike here on page 27 of the *Cours* even if we disagree with the message we're employed to promote. Our job denies us recourse to action. So don't tell me there's no cause for complaint. One might as well tell a rat that laboratory mazes are in principle designed to offer rats alternative pathways, and therefore it is quite unreasonable for the rat to complain that a maze allows it no basis for free action. *My* point was quite different. It was that the choices for talking which any particular linguistic system offers actually constitute that maze. Rats presumably have goals other than running round mazes, even in running round them.'

'Now that's an analogy I can't accept. Linguistic scientists have never held that our linguistic machinery was designed just in order to enable us to run round particular linguistic mazes. I don't know what to call it, but there ought to be a word for a linguistic misrepresentation as crude as that.'

'The glottoconvolutive fallacy, perhaps?'

'Yes, why not?'

'Careful, A. By your own account, we speak the same language. But the word *glottoconvolutive* wasn't in my lexicon. I've never heard of it before.'

'But it *must* have been in your lexicon. For clearly your cerebral linguistic machinery enabled you to produce it when you needed it.'

'And you accepted it, A, even though you have never come across it before either.'

'But that proves my point, B.'

'If you say so. But I think it proves mine.'

'The basic question is: which of us is right?'

'Not necessarily. A more basic question might be whether the answer says anything at all about language.'

*   *   *

All mythology reflects the society which creates it. Other civilisations have had language myths which treated speech as a supernatural gift or attributed magical powers to the written word. But no other civilisation than ours has envisaged language as the product of mysterious inner machinery, run by programs over which human beings have no control. That, it will be said, is just the mythology one might expect of a computer-age society; and so it is. The expectation, nevertheless, risks concealing more than it reveals. Mythologies are as much a reflection of what a society refuses as of what it accepts.

Throughout history revolutions in communications technology have ushered in new concepts of language. The same pattern has repeated itself from the invention of writing onwards. A new and powerful extension of language is introduced, whose salient characteristics are then taken as criterial for all forms of linguistic communication. Thus the advent of writing redefines speech, while the advent of printing redefines both speech and writing. To this pattern of reconceptualisation the computer revolution is no exception. What is significant is that the new view of language promoted is not a conceptual enrichment of what preceded, but a conceptual impoverishment. A society whose academic establishment accepts with alacrity and even with enthusiasm the prospect of being able to treat verbal communication as a complex form of data-processing is a society which proclaims its linguistic immaturity.

The mythology of the language machine is the mythology of a technologically advanced society which has not yet come to terms with its own linguistic self-awareness. It is a society whose linguistic capacities and facilities have fast outgrown its comprehension of them. It is a society which looks in the linguistic mirror, does not like what it sees, and consequently shrinks from its linguistic responsibilities. The signs of its linguistic insecurity are everywhere. It is a society whose words change meaning as they cross frontiers, and whose frontiers are maintained by governments with a right to mint their own truths which is as well established as their right to print their own postage stamps. It is a semantically bemused society in which aggression is always defence, censorship is always exercised in the interests of free speech, and wars are invariably fought to preserve peace. It is a society which proliferates jargon while deploring it, and cares more about the pollution of its rivers by detergents than about the pollution of its communicational space by detergent advertisements. It is a society whose citizens are told that smoking may damage their health but that nuclear power is safe. Its mass media daily produce verbiage for public consumption on a scale never seen before. It is a society of people who have more language to cope with than they can possibly manage, of people ceaselessly bombarded by words they only partly understand. It is a society in which language is increasingly perceived as untrustworthy, and its untrustworthiness increasingly perceived as being without remedy. The typical neurosis of such a society is logophobia. It worries about words while abusing them. No other society could have numbered Orwell among its intellectual heroes, or enacted legislation to enforce 'plain language', or have seen its most popular poet murdered by an admirer who gave as his reason that he understood the words of the poet's lyrics, but not their meaning. In short, it is a society which fears the linguistic jungle it has created because it knows that in jungles only the law of the jungle prevails.

The mythology of the language machine is unique in being able to offer just the psychological placebos which such a society needs. It is a mythology which makes the genetic endowment of *homo sapiens* entirely responsible for how language works, and turns the investigation of its workings into a socially anodyne branch of cognitive studies. At the same time, it allows language to be treated technically on a par with mathematical systems, thus reducing linguistic description to the analysis of formal patterns. It is a mythology which divorces the linguistic form of discourse from its social causes and effects. It tells of linguistic rules buried deep beyond the reach of consciousness, and formulates them in arcane algebras beyond the grasp of lay understanding. In brief, it is a mythology which effectively dehumanises language at the same time as proclaiming language to be the human capacity *par excellence*.

It is a mythology which has already produced solemn absurdities of an order which a latter-day Swift would be hard pressed to satirise. Not even the projectors of the grand academy of Lagado debated such topics as the arithmetic of phoneme counts, or what is the meaning of the sentence *It's five o'clock on the sun*, or how it is logically possible for a child to learn its native language, let alone published their conclusions in learned journals for posterity to marvel at.

The society which feeds and feeds off this mythology is a society in which public communication has manifestly given up on language. Information is a verbal spiral, in which words merely beget other words. The very style of presentation renounces the truth in advance. It is a society which looks into the screened eyes of its newscasters and need look no further than those saccadic responses to understand that one can no longer believe what the President of the United States says about international terrorism, or what the local police say about the protection of the community, or what the news bulletin says about either, or about anything else. What is said is no longer even said to be believed, but to be reported as having been said. The primary function of language is now metalinguistic. Society already reaps the whirlwind of the language machine.

It matters little for the linguistic future of our language-making species whether or not its academic experts belatedly succeed in developing to their own satisfaction a comprehensive 'science of language' in accordance with the canons of whatever philosophy of science happens to be currently fashionable. What is important is that people should come to recognise and understand the mythological processes which language itself engenders. By these linguistic inquiry proceeds, and these it must also transcend. Only then and thus can language makers become language masters, and a society enter into its linguistic inheritance.

Bibliography

J.Ambrose-Grillet, *Glossary of Transformational Grammar*, Rowley 1978.

L.S.Amery, *Thought and Language*, Oxford 1949.

A.R.Anderson (ed.), *Minds and Machines*, Englewood Cliffs 1964.

A.J.Ayer, *Language, Truth and Logic*, London 1936.

E.Bach, *An Introduction to Transformational Grammars*, New York 1964.

G.P.Baker and P.M.S.Hacker, *Language, Sense and Nonsense*, Oxford 1984.

Y.Bar-Hillel, *Language and Information*, Reading, Mass. 1964.

M.Black, *The Labyrinth of Language*, Harmondsworth 1968.

L.Bloomfield, 'Literate and Illiterate Speech', *American Speech*, vol.2, 1927.

R.Boirel, *Le mécanisme hier et aujourd'hui*, Paris 1982.

W.F.Bolton, *The Language of 1984*, Oxford 1984.

G.Boole, *The Mathematical Analysis of Logic*, Cambridge 1847.

P.Bourdieu, *Ce que parler veut dire*, Paris 1982.

D.Cameron, 'What has gender got to do with sex?', *Language & Communication*, vol.5, 1985.

N.Cardus, *Autobiography*, London 1947.

C.Cherry, *On Human Communication*, Cambridge, Mass. 1957.

A.N.Chomsky, *Syntactic Structures*, The Hague 1957.

'A review of B.F.Skinner's *Verbal Behavior*', *Language*, vol.35, 1959. Reprinted in J.A.Fodor and J.J.Katz (eds.), *The Structure of Language*, Englewood Cliffs 1964.

'On the notion "rule of grammar" ', *Proceedings of the Twelfth Symposiun in Applied Mathematics, 1961*. Reprinted in J.A.Fodor and J.J.Katz (eds.), *The Structure of Language*, Englewood Cliffs 1964.

Aspects of the Theory of Syntax, Cambridge, Mass. 1965.

'Knowledge of language: its elements and origins'. In H.C.Longuet-Higgins, J.Lyons and D.E.Broadbent (eds.), *The Psychological Mechanisms of Language*, London 1981.

A.N.Chomsky and M.Halle, *The Sound Pattern of English*, New York 1968.

J.Cohen, *Human Robots in Myth and Science*, London 1966.

W.Churchill, *Beach-la-mar*, Washington 1911.

W.Cobbett, *A Grammar of the English Language*, London 1818.

L.G.Cromwell, 'Bar kar mir. To talk with no curves: important speaking among mainland Torres Strait Islanders', *Anthropological Forum*, vol.5, 1980-2.

D.Crystal, *Introduction to Language Pathology*, London 1980.

  A Dictionary of Linguistics and Phonetics, 2nd ed., Oxford 1985.

E.Delavenay, *An Introduction to Machine Translation*, London 1960.

D.C.Dennett, 'The role of the computer metaphor in understanding the mind', *Computer Culture*, ed. H.R.Pagels, New York 1984.

R.Descartes, *The Philosophical Writings of Descartes*, tr. J.Cottingham, R.Stoothoff and D.Murdoch, Cambridge 1985.

  Discours de la méthode, ed. E.Gilson, 5th ed., Paris 1976.

B.Disraeli, *Sybil*, London 1845.

C.D.Ellis, *Spoken Cree*, 2nd ed., Edmonton, Alberta 1983.

A.Ewert, *The French Language*, London 1933.

P.Feyerabend, *Against Method*, London 1975.

J.A.Fodor, *The Language of Thought*, New York 1975.

J.A.Fodor and J.J.Katz (eds.), *The Structure of Language*, Englewood Cliffs 1964.

R.Fowler, B.Hodge, G.Cress and T.Trew (eds.), *Language and Control*, London 1979.

V.Fromkin and R.Rodman, *An Introduction to Language*, 2nd ed., New York 1978.

J.S.Ganz, *Rules: a Systematic Study*, The Hague 1971.

H.Gardner, *The Mind's New Science*, New York 1985.

A.Gaur, *A History of Writing*, London 1984.

R.L.Gregory, *Mind in Science*, London 1981.

M.Gross and A.Lentin, *Introduction to Formal Grammars*, London 1970.

R.A.Hall, *Leave Your Language Alone*, Ithaca 1950.

R.Harré, *Theories and Things*, London 1961.

R.Harris, *The Language-Makers*, London 1980.
   The Language Myth, London 1981.
   Reading Saussure, London 1987.
Z.S.Harris, *Methods in Structural Linguistics*, Chicago 1951.
A.Hovelacque, *La linguistique*, 2nd ed., Paris 1877.
C.M.Hutton, *The type-token relation: abstraction and instantiation in linguistic theory*, Oxford 1986.
R.Jakobson, 'Two aspects of language and two types of aphasic disturbances'. In R.Jakobson and M.Halle, *Fundamentals of Language*, The Hague 1956.
O.Jespersen, *Essentials of English Grammar*, London 1933.
D.Jones, *An Outline of English Phonetics*, 9th ed., Cambridge 1964.
M.Joos (ed.), *Readings in Linguistics I. The Development of Descriptive Linguistics in America 1925-1956*, Chicago 1966.
J.J.Katz and J.A.Fodor, 'The structure of a semantic theory', *Language*, vol.39, 1963. Reprinted in J.A.Fodor and J.J.Katz (eds.), *The Structure of Language*, Englewood Cliffs 1964. Page references are to the reprint.
J.Leiber, 'The strange creature', *The Meaning of Primate Signals*, ed. R.Harré and V.Reynolds, Cambridge 1984.
W.J.M.Levelt, 'The speaker's linearization problem', *The Psychological Mechanisms of Language*, ed. H.C.Longuet-Higgins, J.Lyons and D.E.Broadbent, London 1981.
G.E.R.Lloyd, *Science and Morality in Greco-Roman Antiquity*, Cambridge 1985.
J.Locke, *An Essay Concerning Human Understanding*, ed. A.C.Fraser, Oxford 1894.
Chief Buffalo Child Long Lance, *Long Lance*, Alberta 1928.
N.Love, 'Making sense of Chomsky's revolution', *Language & Communication*, vol.1, 1981.
J.Lyons, *Introduction to Theoretical Linguistics*, Cambridge 1968.
   Language and Linguistics, Cambridge 1981.
A.Macalister, 'Phrenology', *Encyclopaedia Britannica*, 11th ed., vol.21, Cambridge 1911.
N.Malcolm, 'Moore and ordinary language', *The Philosophy of G.E.Moore*, ed.P.A.Schilpp, New York 1952.
H.Marcuse, *One-Dimensional Man*, London 1964.
M.McLuhan, *The Gutenberg Galaxy*, Toronto 1962.

178   *The Language Machine*

J.Miller, *McLuhan*, London 1971.
G.E.Moore, 'Some judgments of perception', *Proceedings of the Aristotelian Society*, vol.19, 1918.
'A reply to my critics', *The Philosophy of G.E.Moore*, ed. P.A.Schilpp, New York 1952.
P.Mühlhäusler, 'Language and communicational efficiency: the case of Tok Pisin', *Language & Communication*, vol.2, 1982.
'The politics of small languages in Australia and the Pacific', *Language & Communication*, vol.7, 1987.
F.M.Müller, *Lectures on the Science of Language*, London 1861-4.
K.M.E.Murray, *Caught in the Web of Words*, New Haven/London 1977.
W.J.Ong, *Orality and Literacy*, New York 1982.
G.Orwell, *Nineteen Eighty-Four*, London 1949. Page references are to the Penguin Books re-issue, Harmondsworth 1954.
The Collected Essays, Journalism and Letters of George Orwell, ed. S.Orwell and I.Angus, London 1968.
H.R.Pagels (ed.), *Computer Culture*, New York 1984.
D.J.Palmer, *The Rise of English Studies*, Oxford 1965.
F.R.Palmer, *Grammar*, 2nd ed., Harmondsworth 1984.
F.E.Peters, *Greek Philosophical Terms*, New York 1967.
M.K.Pope, *From Latin to Modern French*, Manchester 1934.
H.Putnam, 'Minds and machines', *Dimensions of Mind: A Symposium*, ed. S.Hook, New York 1960. Reprinted in A.R.Anderson (ed.), *Minds and Machines*, Englewood Cliffs 1964.
R.Quirk, S.Greenbaum, G.Leech and J.Svartvik, *A Grammar of Contemporary English*, London 1972.
A.Robinet, *Le langage à l'âge classique*, Paris 1978.
R.H.Robins, *A Short History of Linguistics*, 2nd ed., London 1979.
L.C.Rosenfield, *From Beast-Machine to Man-Machine*, New York 1941.
J.E.Ruby, 'The Origins of Scientific "Law" ', *Journal of the History of Ideas*, vol.47, 1986.
W.J.Samarin, 'The art of Gbeyo insults', *International Journal of American Linguistics*, vol.35, 1969.
E.Sapir, *Language*, New York 1921.
F.de Saussure, *Cours de linguistique générale*, 2nd ed., Paris 1922.

J.R.Searle, *Speech Acts*, Cambridge 1969.

'Minds, brains and programs', *The Behavioral and Brain Sciences*, vol.3, 1980.

C.L.Shannon and W.Weaver, *The Mathematical Theory of Communication*, Urbana 1949.

G.Simons, *Are Computers Alive?*, Brighton 1983.

P.F.Strawson, *Meaning and Truth*, Oxford 1970.

J.Swift, *Gulliver's Travels*, rev. ed., Dublin 1735. Page references are to the text of the Everyman Library edition, London 1940.

A.Tarski, 'The semantic conception of truth', *Philosophy and Phenomenological Research*, vol.4, 1944.

T.J.Taylor, 'Linguistic origins: Bruner and Condillac on learning how to talk', *Language & Communication* vol.4, 1984.

H.S.Terrace, ' "Language" in apes', *The Meaning of Primate Signals*, ed. R.Harré and V.Reynolds, Cambridge 1984.

E.M.W.Tillyard, *The Muse Unchained*, London 1958.

R.C.Trench, *On the Study of Words*, London 1851.

A.M.Turing, 'Computing machinery and intelligence', *Mind*, vol.59, 1950. Reprinted in A.R.Anderson (ed.), *Minds and Machines*, Englewood Cliffs 1964. Page references are to the reprint.

L.S.Vygotsky, *Thought and Language*, Cambridge, Mass. 1962.

J.Weizenbaum, 'ELIZA – A Computer Program for the Study of Natural Language Communication between man and machine', *Communications of the Association for Computing Machinery*, vol.9, 1966.

Computer Power and Human Reason, San Francisco 1976.

A.N.Whitehead, 'Mathematics', *Encyclopaedia Britannica*, 11th ed., vol.17, Cambridge 1911.

W.D.Whitney, *Language and the Study of Language*, 3rd ed., London 1870.

The Life and Growth of Language, 2nd ed., London 1880.

N.Wiener, *Cybernetics*, New York 1948.

J.Z.Young, *Programs of the Brain*, Oxford 1978.

Index